Expanding
TACTICS for LISTENING
THIRD EDITION

Worksheets & Audio Scripts Book

Jack C. Richards
with Grant Trew

More listening. More testing. More effective.

Vocabulary Worksheet 1

Expanding Tactics for Listening Third Edition

Part 1

Use the words in the box to complete the crossword puzzle.

- design
- enough
- introduce
- course
- greet
- ahead
- humid
- remember

Across

1. to plan or create something
3. to have a memory of something
6. a class
7. warm and wet
8. to meet and welcome someone

Down

2. to help someone meet someone else
4. in the front
5. all that is necessary

Vocabulary Worksheet 2

Expanding Tactics for Listening Third Edition

Part 1

Match the words and phrases on the left with their definitions on the right.

1. dangerous
2. hang out
3. instructor
4. careful
5. favorite
6. present
7. paper
8. busy
9. alone
10. visit

A. with a lot of things that you must do
B. a gift
C. risky and possibly harmful
D. a brief stay with others away from home
E. cautious; avoiding harm or injury
F. a teacher or professor
G. a report you write for class
H. being without the company of others
I. to spend free time with friends
J. preferred more than all others

Part 2

Complete the sentences. Use the words or phrases from Part 1.

1. It is important to be _____ when driving on icy roads.
2. I met my friends at the mall so we could just _____ .
3. His parents were out of town, leaving him _____ for the weekend.
4. She was very _____ with her many afterschool activities.
5. The _____ was strict in class, but very friendly outside of school.
6. At Christmas, I bought a _____ for my friend.
7. The assignment was to write a _____ about the American Civil War.
8. During the summer, I like to _____ my grandparents for a week.
9. His _____ sport used to be hockey, but now he thinks soccer is the best.
10. Fearing injury, the hikers said the mountain trail was too _____ .

Vocabulary Worksheet 3

Expanding Tactics for Listening Third Edition

Part 1

Find the words in the box in the word search puzzle.

atmosphere	comfortable
popular	stylist
staff	quality
service	speed
rude	website

```
V D E E P S B J U C
A B Q G F H P K T O
N T S U F W E R Y M
Q D M P A O U M F F
Y S E O T L J G X O
L T T P S V I B R R
N Y I U C P R T D T
R L S L K M H V Y A
I I B A R U D E G B
N S E R V I C E R L
F T W O H E B Y J E
```

Part 2

Complete the sentences. Use the words from Part 1.

1. This new mattress is much more _____ than the old one.

2. The runner will win the marathon if he can maintain his _____ .

3. With such thoughtful servers, it's no wonder the _____ is great.

4. The dim lighting and soft music give the restaurant a great _____ .

5. Jim was hired as a member of the company's sales _____ .

6. We should really tip the valet, so we don't seem _____ .

7. The fresh seafood arrives daily, so it is of the very best _____ .

8. My _____ always gives me great haircuts.

9. The _____ offered the option of tracking my diet online.

10. The _____ kids are known by everyone at school.

Vocabulary Worksheet 4

Expanding Tactics for Listening Third Edition

Look at the words and the definitions below. Make a sentence using each word.

Word	Definition	My sentence
worry	to be concerned about something	
scratch	a depression cut into a surface	
dozen	12 of something	
occasion	an important event	
tripped	fell over something	
on time	at the expected time	
break down	to stop working; usually refers to a car	
directions	an explanation of how to get to someplace	
accident	something that happens suddenly or by chance, often with bad results	
unusual	not normal or ordinary	
graduation	a ceremony for people who have completed a high school, college or university degree	
neighbors	people who live very near each other	

Vocabulary Worksheet 5

Expanding Tactics for Listening Third Edition

Part 1

Use the words in the box to complete the crossword puzzle.

enthusiastic
intelligent
patient
strict
criticized
praise
athletic
depressed
bother

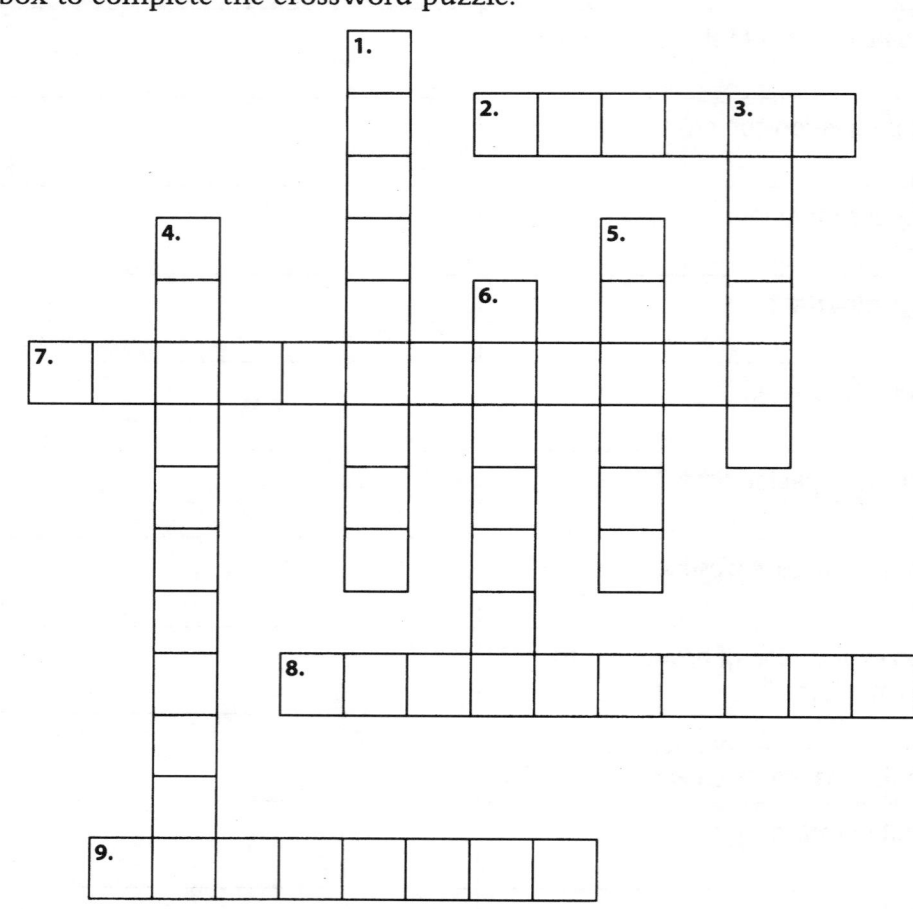

Across

2. to compliment someone
7. cheerful; eager
8. judged; looked for faults
9. fit, healthy, and active

Down

1. feeling sad and hopeless
3. closely following and enforcing the rules
4. smart; informed
5. to trouble oneself
6. able to stay calm when you are waiting

Vocabulary Worksheet 6

Expanding Tactics for Listening Third Edition

Part 1

Read the definitions and unscramble the words below.

| baggage | platform | departure | passengers | delayed | arrival | exhausted | flight | refreshments | seat belt |

1. Very tired
   dehusxateu _____

2. The place where you board a train
   fropmalt _____

3. Beginning later than planned
   ledayde _____

4. Snacks such as sodas and chips
   thremrefsens _____

5. A person riding on a bus, train, or airplane
   gaspsenser _____

6. Leaving a place
   perdarute _____

7. What travelers keep their belongings in
   gabegag _____

8. A single, specific trip on an airplane
   ghilft _____

9. A device to hold passengers to their chairs
   blasteet _____

10. Coming to a place
    raviral _____

Part 2

Complete the sentences. Use the words from Part 1.

1. After the plane landed, I picked up my _____ at the carousel.
2. The flight attendant asked me to fasten my _____.
3. After waiting to leave for an hour, the plane was finally ready for _____.
4. I was so _____ when I arrived that I fell right to sleep.
5. She asked an attendant which _____ the train would arrive at.
6. Because of the bad weather, the flight had to be _____.
7. On the flight, people were offered _____ instead of a full meal.
8. Having shown up early, I patiently waited for the train's _____.
9. The plane was so full of _____ that there were no empty seats.
10. The _____ to Sydney was very long and boring.

© Oxford University Press. Permission granted to reproduce for classroom use.   Vocabulary Worksheets

Vocabulary Worksheet 7

Expanding Tactics for Listening Third Edition

Part 1

Match the words and phrases on the left with their definitions on the right.

1. suburbs
2. annoying
3. yard
4. commuting
5. ancient
6. single
7. convenient
8. condition
9. maintenance
10. appliances

A. traveling to work
B. the grassy area around a house
C. household machines, like a dishwasher or an oven
D. cleaning, repairing, and taking care of something
E. smaller towns that surround a big city
F. the state that a house or car is in
G. very old
H. making you a little angry
I. simple, easy, and useful
J. not in a romantic relationship

Complete the sentences. Use the words from Part 1.

1. After the accident, the car was in very bad _____.
2. The old apartment was falling apart, and required constant _____.
3. I decided to leave the city for a quiet life in the _____.
4. For a while, I was _____ to the office by train.
5. He visited Greece to see all the _____ buildings from long ago.
6. The store was very _____, since it was only a block from his apartment.
7. She found her neighbor's frequent visits to be _____.
8. She decided to buy all new _____ for the kitchen.
9. After years of dating different people, somehow she was still _____.
10. After lunch, we should go outside and play football in the _____.

Vocabulary Worksheets   © Oxford University Press. Permission granted to reproduce for classroom use.

Vocabulary Worksheet 8

Expanding Tactics for Listening Third Edition

Part 1

Find the words in the box in the word search puzzle.

ghost	plumbing
ingredients	stadium
neglect	elaborate
tuition	identify
column	scam

```
G  Y  S  T  A  D  I  U  M  I
P  U  J  N  E  S  V  A  K  N
E  L  A  B  O  R  A  T  E  G
I  C  U  X  G  H  W  C  X  R
T  B  O  M  F  U  L  T  V  E
U  R  D  L  B  V  X  S  Y  D
I  N  R  G  U  I  P  O  K  I
T  P  S  C  A  M  N  H  B  E
I  S  K  B  Q  L  N  G  I  N
O  T  Y  N  E  G  L  E  C  T
N  I  D  E  N  T  I  F  Y  S
Q  G  K  O  J  E  S  T  M  R
```

Part 2

Complete the sentences. Use the words from Part 1.

1. I need to go shopping to get the _____ for this recipe.
2. Despite all the clues, the police could not _____ the criminal.
3. Because the building was old, the _____ often leaked.
4. The old woman claimed to see the _____ of her dead husband.
5. Without regular servicing, the car fell into a state of _____.
6. The _____ for this university is very expensive.
7. The concert was so big, it had to be held in a _____.
8. The decorations for the princess's wedding were incredibly _____.
9. Don't reply to that email; it is clearly just a _____.
10. I read a very interesting _____ in this morning's newspaper.

Vocabulary Worksheet 9

Expanding Tactics for Listening Third Edition

Part 1

Use the words in the box to complete the crossword puzzle.

- autograph
- education
- appearance
- director
- diet
- festival
- crowds
- craft

Across

2. the way something looks
5. a big party or celebration
6. a job or activity for which you need skill with your hands
7. large groups of people
8. the foods that a person eats regularly

Down

1. a person's handwritten signature
3. the process of learning
4. a manager or supervisor (sometimes for actors)

Vocabulary Worksheet 10

Expanding Tactics for Listening Third Edition

Look at the words and the definitions below. Make a sentence using each word.

Word	Definition	My sentence
documentary	a film or television program about real-life events	
sitcom	a television program about people in a funny situation	
soap opera	a television program about romance and relationship drama	
hurricane	a storm with very strong winds	
episode	one part in a television series	
miserable	experiencing extreme unhappiness	
defense	protection from harm	
impression	a quick judgment based mostly on outward appearances	
breakthrough	an important discovery, as in research or an investigation	
contestant	a person who competes on a game show	
hilarious	very funny	
trivia	very specific facts about a particular subject	

Vocabulary Worksheet 11

Expanding Tactics for Listening Third Edition

Part 1

Read the definitions and unscramble the words below.

| culture | nightlife | safety | traffic | clubs | crime | sightseeing | musicians | wallet | relieved |

1. free from worrying about something
   leriveed _____
2. all kinds of fun activities after dark
   genthilif _____
3. taking a tour and visiting landmarks
   sestigehing _____
4. people who play instruments or write music
   acismunis _____
5. places to dance and hear music
   bulcs _____
6. an action that is against the law
   mecir _____
7. freedom from harm or injury
   festay _____
8. a place to keep money and credit cards
   lawtel _____
9. the ways and customs of a people
   ructule _____
10. all the cars on the road
    fractif _____

Part 2

Complete the sentences. Use words from Part 1.

1. We listened to the _____ play beautiful songs in the street.
2. There was a lot of _____ on the road, so I was late for dinner.
3. We decided to go dancing at the _____ on my birthday.
4. Studying abroad is a great way to learn a lot about a different _____.
5. A thief stole my _____.
6. With so many tourist attractions, we spent the whole day just _____.
7. I was _____ when I found the papers I thought I'd lost.
8. The man committed a _____ by breaking into his neighbor's house.
9. The _____ in Tokyo is amazing, with so many dance clubs and concerts.
10. _____ is a major concern in the city, where crime can be high.

Vocabulary Worksheet 12

Expanding Tactics for Listening Third Edition

Part 1

Match the words and phrases on the left with their definitions on the right.

1. economy
2. fence
3. industry
4. factory
5. club
6. business
7. out of business
8. public transportation
9. deserted
10. inexperienced

A. a group for people with the same interests
B. a facility for manufacturing goods
C. lacking knowledge, training, or involvement
D. people or companies that produce and sell goods
E. totally empty of people
F. a barrier
G. having to do with money, business, and sales
H. a single money-making enterprise
I. means of mass travel, such as trains, subways, and buses
J. no longer in operation

Part 2

Complete the sentences. Use the words or phrases from Part 1.

1. I use _____ to get around the city because I don't have a car.
2. No one was in the building when he arrived; it was completely _____.
3. My first _____ was an Internet company that I started while I was in school.
4. No one would hire the young man because he was still _____.
5. In college, I belonged to a _____ devoted to movies and filmmaking.
6. After several banks and companies closed, the _____ began to worsen.
7. The company built a new _____ to produce its new line of cars.
8. Having lost too much money, the company finally went _____.
9. I built a tall _____ around my yard so I could have privacy from my neighbors.
10. With more _____ in the area, there would be more jobs.

© Oxford University Press. Permission granted to reproduce for classroom use.   Vocabulary Worksheets

Vocabulary Worksheet 13

Expanding Tactics for Listening Third Edition

Part 1

Find the words in the box in the word search puzzle.

bother	fan
honor	anniversary
admission	romantic
celebrate	midnight
invite	valentine

G N T V A L E N T I N E
P I C H D I W U B L O M
R X O G M N B M I C P I
O C B A I V R P E H F D
M U O J S I K F O F T N
A P T H S T F N I A L I
N F H W I E O S X N B G
T R E Q O R L T E T J H
I V R R N K L D V Y O T
C K H E T A R B E L E C
Y R A S NR EI V I N N A O

Part 2

Complete the sentences. Use the words from Part 1.

1. On Sundays, _____ to the Natural History Museum is free.
2. They threw a big party for their parents' fiftieth wedding _____.
3. My girlfriend and I enjoyed a _____ dinner at an Italian restaurant.
4. On Memorial Day, Americans _____ soldiers who died in wars.
5. Are you going to _____ a lot of guests to the party?
6. After we won the soccer match, we decided to go out and _____.
7. Look how late it is; it's past _____!
8. Please be quiet, so we don't _____ our neighbors.
9. I sent a card, some chocolates, and a red rose to my special _____.
10. Mia is a big _____ of Halloween, because she loves to wear costumes.

Vocabulary Worksheet 14

Expanding Tactics for Listening Third Edition

Part 1

Use the words in the box to complete the crossword puzzle.

- formal
- elegant
- handsome
- trousers
- typical
- blouse
- promotion
- plain
- imported

Across

1. simple; lacking style
4. getting a higher position at work
5. a shirt worn by women
7. wearing very nice clothes (as to a wedding)
8. being good-looking (usually refers to men)
9. normal; ordinary

Down

2. made in and sold from another country
3. long pants
6. refined; neat; graceful

Vocabulary Worksheet 15

Expanding Tactics for Listening Third Edition

Look at the words and the definitions below. Make a sentence using each word.

Word	Definition	My sentence
useful	being of use; practical and helpful	
rather	used to express a preference for one thing over another	
kind of	slightly; somewhat	
delicious	tasting very good	
work on	to fix or repair something	
background	a person's previous experience or training	
make sense	to be logical and easy to understand	
position	a job ins a company with specific responsibilities	
trendy	in fashion	
disturbed	bothered; interrupted	
housekeeping	a service offered by a hotel for the purpose of cleaning hotel rooms	
guide	one who leads, as on a tour	

Vocabulary Worksheet 16

Expanding Tactics for Listening Third Edition

Part 1

Read the definitions and unscramble the words below.

| appointment | congratulations | remind | suggestion | request | absent | damage | tied up | pleased | scared |

1. to help someone remember something

    nimerd _____

2. to break or cause harm to something

    magade _____

3. an agreed-on date to meet with someone

    noptampient _____

4. an idea that is recommended

    gistugenso _____

5. to be busy doing something

    udit pe _____

6. an expression of happiness for someone else's good fortune

    rastioncuglotan _____

7. not there

    nsaetb _____

8. satisfied with something

    saplede _____

9. to ask for something

    sterque _____

10. afraid

    dercas _____

Part 2

Complete the sentences. Use the words from Part 1.

1. Did the accident _____ your car?
2. I am _____ of flying, so I usually take the train.
3. Mike was very _____ with the good grade he got on the test.
4. She offered her _____ to John when she heard about his raise.
5. At the meeting, I made a _____ about how to improve sales.
6. I was running late for my _____ with the doctor.
7. Jason was so _____ with schoolwork that he didn't have time to eat.
8. Ann was _____ from school because she had a cold.
9. She promised to _____ me to take out the garbage if I forgot.
10. I had to _____ another application, since I spilled coffee on the first.

Vocabulary Worksheet 17

Expanding Tactics for Listening Third Edition

Part 1

Match the words and phrases on the left with their definitions on the right.

1. valuable
2. exactly
3. alarm
4. injured
5. pajamas
6. nervous
7. suddenly
8. realize
9. elevator
10. luckily

A. to have one's expectations unmet
B. without warning
C. to become aware of something
D. worth a lot of money
E. precisely; very accurately
F. easily excitable; anxious
G. a device that signals a bad event
H. fortunately
I. a machine that takes people up and down between floors in a building

Part 2

Complete the sentences. Use the words or phrases from Part 1

1. Please put on your _____ and get into bed.
2. My grandmother left me a pearl necklace that is very _____.
3. _____, your leg isn't broken.
4. I will not pay for food if it is not _____ what I ask for.
5. He was very _____ at the thought of giving a presentation for the boss.
6. I took the _____ to the 14th floor, since the stairs took too long.
7. _____, the car burst into flames while driving down the road.
8. I have an _____ that goes off when someone enters the house.
9. After waking up with a fever, I _____ that I should see the doctor.
10. He _____ his knee when he was playing soccer.

Vocabulary Worksheet 18

Expanding Tactics for Listening Third Edition

Part 1

Find the words in the box in the word search puzzle.

safari	plays
jungle	backpacker
galleries	fascinating
resort	free
practice	on my own

```
F  P  G  A  L  L  E  R  I  E  S
A  R  I  V  P  L  A  Y  S  K  B
S  A  F  A  R  I  N  G  D  V  A
C  C  H  R  E  S  O  R  T  J  C
I  T  B  O  L  A  Z  V  P  V  K
N  I  T  N  E  L  G  N  U  J  P
A  C  V  M  D  B  I  E  Q  M  A
T  E  B  Y  Q  H  D  A  S  Y  C
I  N  R  O  F  R  E  E  U  R  K
N  F  Y  W  C  M  G  D  Y  C  E
G  M  T  N  E  Q  A  K  L  F  R
```

Part 2

Complete the sentences. Use the words from Part 1.

1. While usually quite boring, today's astronomy lecture was actually _____.

2. We went to lots of museums and art _____ during our vacation.

3. We don't have much money, so we like to go to _____ concerts.

4. The hostel in Berlin was a great place to stay for a penniless _____ like me.

5. I'll never become a famous musician if I don't _____ every day.

6. On our trip to the Caribbean, everything we needed was right there at the _____.

7. The best part of our trip was the day we went on a _____ in the savanna.

8. I love theater, so I go to _____ often.

9. At the hotel in Borneo, we could hear noises coming from the nearby _____ all night long.

10. I decided that I would be happier _____ than with a group of people.

© Oxford University Press. Permission granted to reproduce for classroom use.   Vocabulary Worksheets

Vocabulary Worksheet 19

Expanding Tactics for Listening Third Edition

Part 1

Use the words in the box to complete the crossword puzzle.

- suffer
- entertainment
- magazine
- politics
- theft
- escape
- rescued
- protest

Across

2. to get out of a bad situation
4. yo experience something bad
7. amusing activity for fun

Down

1. stealing
3. the study of government
5. to show disagreement
6. saved from danger
8. a weekly or monthly publication that contains pictures, articles, and stories

Vocabulary Worksheet 20

Expanding Tactics for Listening Third Edition

Look at the words and the definitions below. Make a sentence using each word.

Word	Definition	My sentence
companion	a friend who spends a lot time with you	
informative	providing useful facts	
pride	a feeling of respect for oneself	
commercials	advertisements on TV or radio	
distracting	taking one's attention away from more important matters	
develop	to build up unused land or neighborhoods	
allowed	given permission to do something	
encourage	to inspire someone to have confidence	
interrupt	to distract someone from a conversation or activity	
universe	everything that exists anywhere	
violent	forceful, aggressive, and often harmful	
absolutely	without any doubt	

Vocabulary Worksheet 21

Expanding Tactics for Listening Third Edition

Part 1

Read the definitions and unscramble the words below.

| famous | invent | athlete | scientist | advertisement | newcomer | inspired | prison | elected | retired |

1. someone who is good at sports

   teelaht _____

2. where most criminals are sent

   nposir _____

3. to create something entirely new

   nevtin _____

4. encouraged to act by someone or something

   repsindi _____

5. voted into a government office

   teclede _____

6. a new participant in some activity

   menworec _____

7. extremely popular among many people

   somafu _____

8. no longer working, by choice

   tredire _____

9. a way of promoting a product in media

   esitnamdevret _____

10. someone who studies biology, physics, or similar subjects

    cinetsits _____

Part 2

Complete the sentences. Use the words from Part 1.

1. Martin wanted to _____ something totally new.
2. The thief was sent to _____ for his crimes.
3. On his first day at school, the _____ was welcomed by his classmates.
4. Jessica often dreams of becoming a _____ actor.
5. The director's latest film was _____ by his trip to Africa.
6. The _____ was busy doing research in his laboratory.
7. After 30 years of hard work, Frank finally _____ from his business.
8. A professional _____ must train many hours every day to stay strong.
9. The _____ made Lisa want to buy the new product.
10. On Tuesday, the people voted and _____ a new prime minister.

Vocabulary Worksheet 22

Expanding Tactics for Listening Third Edition

Look at the words and the definitions below. Make a sentence using each word.

Word	Definition	My sentence
poultry	a type of meat including many birds like chicken, turkey, duck	
dessert	an often sweet dish served at the end of a meal	
sodium	a mineral and nutrient from which salt comes	
cholesterol	a natural substance produced by the body that can become dangerous if levels rise too high	
pyramid	a shape or structure with triangular sides and a flat base	
vitamin	a substance that provides required nutrition to the body	
cultivated	having promoted the growth of something, like plants or crops	
fermentation	a process that is used to make alcohol and pickled foods	
pay attention	to focus on (something)	
ripe	fully developed; ready to be eaten (in the case of plants)	
mature	to reach full growth or development	
blood pressure	the force of blood pushing on blood vessel walls; can be dangerous if too high or too low	

Vocabulary Worksheet 23

Expanding Tactics for Listening Third Edition

Part 1

Match the words and phrases on the left with their definitions on the right.

1. predicament
2. cheated
3. aware
4. borrow
5. forget
6. apologize
7. unfortunately
8. awkward
9. anonymous
10. weird

A. having knowledge or understanding of something
B. unluckily
C. very strange
D. a difficult situation with no easy solution
E. to take something from someone for a limited time
F. to be unable to remember
G. uncomfortable or embarrassing
H. did something that is not honest or fair
I. to say you are sorry
J. having no known identity

Part 2

Complete the sentences. Use words from Part 1.

1. I had to _____ to my friend for ruining her favorite shirt.
2. David's mother was very disappointed when she found out that he had _____ on the test.
3. _____, the sudden rainstorm caused the game to be cancelled.
4. When walking alone at night, it is important to be _____ of your surroundings.
5. My friend has been acting _____ lately, and I'm worried about him.
6. Unable to identify the donor, the foundation accepted the _____ donation.
7. Being in the middle of a fight between friends is a terrible _____.
8. We had nothing to talk about, so our first date was kind of _____.
9. He wrote himself a note so he wouldn't _____ his wife's birthday.
10. My neighbor asked to _____ my power tools for two or three days.

Vocabulary Worksheet 24

Expanding Tactics for Listening Third Edition

Part 1

Use the words in the box to complete the crossword puzzle.

pollution
poverty
issue
bombs
chemicals
freeways
garbage
landfills
megacities

Across

1. exploding devices
4. harmful substances in the air and water
5. waste material
7. large roads for fast traffic
8. places to bury waste

Down

2. an important topic
3. solid or liquid materials that can be unsafe (often found in industrial waste)
4. the state of being very poor
6. extremely large cities

Audio Scripts

Unit 1: Small Talk

page 2, CD 1-2
Listening 1

1.
A: Hi. I don't think we've met, have we?
B: No, I don't think so. My name's Mia.
A: Nice to meet you, Mia. I'm Tim Clark.

2.
A: Hey, you're Mike Thompson, right?
B: That's right. And you're Jenny.
A: Yeah! Jenny Lindsay.
B: Yeah, right. We met at Jake's wedding.
A: It's great to see you again!
B: Great to see you, too!

3.
A: Haven't we met somewhere?
B: No, I don't think so.
A: Aren't you Kevin Grant?
B: No, my name is Greg. Greg Brown.
A: Oh, I'm sorry. I was positive we'd met before.

4.
A: Jeff! Hi. Remember me?
B: Sue? Sue Thomas?
A: That's right. We were in that computer class together.
B: Yeah. Boy, was that class boring!
A: Sure was. So how've you been?
B: Pretty good, thanks.

5.
A: Oh, hi. You're Jonathan, aren't you?
B: Yes, and you're Wendy.
A: Yeah. We met at the conference in Hawaii last summer.
B: Right. Nice to see you again.
A: Nice to see you, too.

6.
A: Hi! Don't we work in the same building?
B: Yes, I think we do.
A: I'm Gary James. I'm in accounting.
B: Hi. I'm Lynn Williams. I'm in marketing.

page 3, CD 1-3
Listening 2

1.
A: Hey, Annie, that looks really nice on you. Is it new?
B: Yeah, I got it on sale at George Brothers Department Store. I never miss their sales. They've got really good prices.
A: Well, you made a good choice. That color looks great.
B: Thanks.
A: Oh! Look at the time. I didn't realize it was so late. I've got to run. Good seeing you!

2.
A: What are you taking this year?
B: Mostly literature courses.
A: Oh, really. Are they any good?
B: Some of them are. Except for Professor Scott's class. I mean, the books are interesting, and the lectures are great, but his tests are so hard.
A: Really? Are they essay or short answer tests?

3.
A: What an awful month we are having.
B: It's pretty bad, isn't it? So hot and humid. It's hard to sleep at night, too. I wish I had air conditioning.
A: Me, too.
B: Funny, it's not usually this hot in the fall.
A: That's true. Well, I think I'm going to get some more chips. Enjoy the party!

4.
A: So tell me, Kim. What's he like?
B: Well, he's really fun to be with. He always says funny things and makes me laugh.
A: He sounds really nice.
B: He is. And he's always giving me little presents. But I guess the gifts will stop when he knows me better.
A: Yeah, probably. So how long have you known him, anyway?

5.
A: So, are you still doing the same thing, David?
B: Yeah, I am, unfortunately. I wish I was doing something more challenging.
A: So why don't you look for something else?
B: I really should. I feel stuck in that office because I'm not moving ahead. That's the worst thing about it.
A: Well, good luck to you. If I hear about any jobs, I'll let you know.

6.
A: So, everybody's fine at home, Sarah?
B: Yes, they are, thanks. Oh, some exciting news! My sister Jenny's getting married!
A: Really? When?
B: Next month. She's marrying a guy she met when she was studying in Canada, and we're all going to Toronto for the wedding. It'll be fun.
A: Sounds great. And how about your brother? What's he been doing lately?

page 4, CD 1-4
Listening 3

1.
Yes, I do. I really enjoy living here. So far everything has been fine. The downtown area is really pretty, and I love all the cafes and restaurants there. The other thing I like is that the town's small, so it's easy to get to know people.

2.
Yes, I do. It's a very difficult language to learn, but I guess all languages are difficult. I tried to learn Japanese once, and it was really hard. These days, though, it's easier to learn a foreign language because you can buy some fantastic courses online and on DVD.

3.
I have two children, a girl and a boy. They're both going to school, so they keep us very busy. My husband comes from a big family and would love to have more children, but I think two is enough.

4.
I have a small design company. We design menus, calendars, and things like that. There are just three of us in the company. Last year was a very quiet year for us, but it looks as if business is really improving this year. Would you like to visit our office sometime?

5.
Oh yeah, I've been having a great time since I arrived. Everyone's been very helpful, and I've made some wonderful new friends. I still have a few more days here, so I'm thinking of renting a car and driving up to the mountains.

6.
I'm from a town called Cairns, on the northeast coast of Australia. It's a small town, but I enjoying living there. It's not far from the Great Barrier Reef, which is one of the most famous places in Australia. You should go there sometime.

page 5, CD 1-5
Pronunciation

1. Where does he go to school?
2. I have to call his teacher.
3. What's her job?
4. Have you known him for a long time?

page 5, CD 1-6
Dictation

A: Hi, haven't we met before?
B: Yeah, I think we met at Kate's wedding.
A: That's right! Have you seen her lately?

B: No, I haven't seen her in months. But I talked with her husband last week.
A: Oh, really? How's he doing?
B: He's doing really well. He told me that he got a great new job.
A: I'm happy to hear that. Well, I've got to go, but it was great to see you.
B: Yeah, you, too! If you see John again, tell him I said hello.

Unit 2: Plans

page 6, CD 1–7
Listening 1

1.
A: You're excited about next December, aren't you?
B: Yes, I really am. I can hardly wait!
A: What exactly are you planning to do?
B: My friend and I are going on a cruise in the Caribbean.

2.
A: Your family's going to Florida next summer, aren't they?
B: I'm not really sure where they're planning to go.
A: You're going with them, aren't you?
B: Of course. I wouldn't miss learning to sail for anything!

3.
A: I heard you and two friends are going on a long drive next May.
B: Yeah, I'm getting a newer car to drive across Canada.
A: You'll be visiting Vancouver, won't you?
B: Oh, yeah, we're excited about visiting there. It's supposed to be beautiful!

4.
A: Do you have any idea what you're doing next August?
B: Well, we've been talking about going to the beach.
A: You really love the ocean, don't you?
B: Yeah, but I think this year I'm going to play golf instead.

5.
A: What can we do next summer?
B: Well, we could take a course at the university.
A: You wouldn't want to do that, would you? You work so hard all year long.
B: You're right. How about if we both work in a camp?

6.
A: You're not going to learn to ski next winter, are you?
B: Why not? It sounds very exciting to me!
A: It sounds rather dangerous to me.
B: I'll be careful. Besides, the instructor will be right there to help me if I fall down.

page 7, CD 1–8
Listening 2

1.
A: Hey, Mark. How's it going?
B: Pretty good, how about you?
A: I'm good, thanks. So, what are you up to this weekend?
B: Sam and I are going to a baseball game at the new stadium.
A: Wow! Really? Have a great time!

2.
A: Hey, Jennifer. You're planning to go to Steven's party this weekend, aren't you?
B: No. I really want to go, but I can't.
A: Oh no! Why not?
B: I have to go out of town with my parents. We're going to visit my aunt in Chicago. And we're driving the whole way!

3.
A: So, what are your plans this weekend, Angela?
B: Well, on Saturday, I'm going to the beach with some friends. How about you?
A: I'm going to the beach, too! Maybe I'll see you there. Are you going to Baker Beach?
B: No, we're going to Stinson Beach.
A: Oh. Well, maybe my friends won't mind changing plans.

4.
A: So, I'll see you later, John.
B: Yeah, I'll probably see you at the library tomorrow.
A: Really? But you usually play basketball on Saturdays, don't you?
B: Yeah, but we're not playing this Saturday.
A: Why not?
B: We always take a week off for final exams. I'm planning on studying all weekend.

5.
A: Got any fun plans for the weekend?
B: I have to work most of the weekend, but I'm going out on Friday night.
A: Where are you going?
B: My friends and I are going to go out to dinner. We're going to try that new Mexican restaurant on Branch Street. I hear it's great.

6.
A: What are you doing this weekend, Ji-hyun?
B: I don't have any plans for Saturday, but I'm going shopping on Sunday.
A: You're going to the mall, aren't you?
B: No, I'm going to go downtown. I like the stores better there.

page 8, CD 1–9
Listening 3

1.
I have a really busy weekend ahead of me. I have to work about ten hours on Saturday. I'm really excited about Saturday night, though. I'm going to my friend Alex's party. He always has great parties. I don't have to go to work on Sunday, but I do have to spend all morning and afternoon writing a paper for my history class. Then on Sunday night, I'm going to the movies with some friends.

2.
This is going to be a great weekend. I can't wait for Sunday afternoon! My soccer team is playing in the finals! I hope we win! On Saturday, I'm going to the beach with my friends. And on Saturday night, we're going to have dinner at my favorite restaurant.

3.
I don't really have a lot going on this weekend. I was so busy last weekend that I didn't want to make any big plans for this weekend. I played soccer and went hiking last Saturday, then went for a long bike ride on Sunday. This weekend, I'm just going to stay home and read a book. I'm excited about being home by myself and relaxing all weekend.

4.
My friends and I are taking a road trip to Los Angeles this weekend. We're planning on leaving on Friday after class. We'll get to LA at around 7:00 in the evening—just in time for dinner. On Saturday, we'll probably hang out at the beach during the day. We're going to have a fire and sing songs all night. It's going to be fantastic.

5.
I plan to study most of this weekend, but on Saturday evening, I'm going over to my friend's house. It's her birthday, so she's having a few friends over for dinner. I'm really looking forward to seeing her! We haven't seen each other in two months! I knew I wouldn't have time to go shopping on Saturday, so I bought her a birthday gift on Friday. I got her a sweater. I hope she likes it!

6.
I play the guitar in a band, and my band has two shows this weekend. We're playing in a little cafe on Sunday night. We play there a lot and have a lot of fans there, so it'll be fun. I'm really excited about Saturday night, though. We're playing at a club downtown. We've never played in a big club before, so I'm kind of nervous.

page 9, CD 1-10
Pronunciation
1. You made a reservation, didn't you?
2. She's in your class, isn't she?
3. He's driving, isn't he?
4. We're busy Friday, aren't we?

page 9, CD 1-11
Dictation
A: Do you want to play soccer this Saturday?
B: It's supposed to rain this weekend, isn't it?
A: Oh, I didn't know that. Well, then what do you want to do?
B: We could go to a movie? We could go see the new action movie.
A: You saw that movie last weekend, didn't you?
B: Yeah, but I'd like to see it again. But you don't like action movies, do you?
A: Not really.
B: We could go see that new comedy at Star Cinema!

Unit 3: Successful Businesses

page 10, CD 1-12
Listening 1
1.
A: What's the new Indian restaurant on Sixth Street like?
B: Well, everyone said it was very good, but I wasn't too satisfied when I went there the other night.
A: Why not?
B: The food was good, but it took too long to arrive. We had to wait for nearly an hour before we got anything to eat.
A: Oh! That's terrible service.

2.
A: I'm going to get the textbook for our biology class at the campus bookstore. Do you want to come?
B: No, I don't think so.
A: Why not? Don't you think it's convenient having a bookstore right on campus?
B: Yes, it is. But have you compared their prices with other bookstores? That store in the mall is usually about 10% cheaper. And you save about 20% buying your books online.
A: Oh. I didn't know that.

3.
A: Do you belong to a health club?
B: Not right now. I used to go to the Metropolitan Health Club on Third Street. I thought it was great because it was so cheap, but then I stopped going.
A: Really? I heard it was pretty popular.
B: That was the problem. It was too popular. It was always full of people. Sometimes I had to wait a long time to use the machines.

4.
A: So how was the hotel in Honolulu?
B: It was pretty good. The staff was really nice—very friendly and helpful. There was one problem with it, though.
A: What was that?
B: The location. It was too far from the restaurants and clubs. Next time, I think I'll stay much closer to the downtown.

5.
A: Do you want to try Italian food tonight?
B: Sure. Where would you like to go?
A: How about Little Roma—you know, that Italian restaurant across from the movie theater? I heard the prices are cheap.
B: That's true. But the service is pretty bad. The waiters are really slow, and they're not very friendly either.
A: Oh, I didn't know that. Let's try another place.

6.
A: I heard there's a sale at Brenda's Boutique. Do you want to check it out? They have some really good clothes.
B: I know, but the service is terrible. The people who work there are so rude.
A: I know what you mean.

page 11, CD 1-13
Listening 2
1.
I really enjoy going there with friends after work. There's always something interesting on the menu. I also love the atmosphere. It's very cool and they have really comfortable sofas.

2.
I'm glad I decided to study there. My Spanish is much better now. It's pretty expensive, but the facilities are very good. They have a great computer lab, and there's free wifi all over campus. It's much better than the school I was going to last year.

3.
I've been going there for over a year. I just love the way they make my hair look. The stylists are really good at their work. The atmosphere makes you feel at home, too, with coffee and snacks, plus really good music. Sure, it's expensive, but I only go there every two months or so.

4.
It's a great place to stay. The atmosphere is so glamorous and exciting. There are bright lights at the front door, and people always arrive in really expensive cars. The rooms are really beautiful, too. Of course, it's not the cheapest hotel in Miami, but it's definitely the best.

5.
I always take mine to a garage on Market Street. It takes a long time to get there from my house, but it's worth the trip. It's the best repair shop in the city. The mechanics do great work, and they never try to charge you too much. In fact, the prices are great—about half the cost of some other places in town.

6.
I get most of my shirts there. You'll love the store. All of their stuff looks great and fits perfectly. It's really good quality, too. They also have lots of different styles and colors to choose from. The window displays are a problem, though. They aren't well-lit, so it's hard to see what they have from outside the store.

page 12, CD 1-14
Listening 3
1.
I think the most important thing is service. If customers feel like they are treated poorly, then they probably won't come back. That's why I train all of my workers to give excellent service. They greet customers politely, show them to a table right away, and explain the items on the menu. Of course, the food is important, too. The fish has to be as fresh as possible, and you have to find talented chefs to prepare it.

2.
The Internet has totally changed this business. In the old days, people *had* to come to a travel agency to get tickets. Now they go online and get their tickets by themselves. When they come to me, I know they're looking for a good value. That's really the most important thing. Of course, our travel agency provides convenience for some clients who don't have the time to plan their own trips.

3.
These days, nothing is more important than speed. Time is money. People want a job done well, but they want it done quickly. And they're usually prepared to pay a little more if you can promise it will get done fast. And, of course, quality is important, too. We're building people's homes, so we want them to enjoy living there for a long time.

4.
It's so important to have the right kind of displays. Creating effective clothing displays is an art. You want people to see the items right away, pick them up, touch them, and then go try the clothes on. And you want them to buy something, too! Good prices are also important, but the display is really the number one thing.

page 13, CD 1–15
Pronunciation

1. The food took too long to arrive.
2. They were not professional.
3. The prices are really high.
4. The waiters were really slow.
5. That hotel is too far from the restaurants and clubs.
6. The rooms are not nice.

page 13, CD 1–16
Dictation

A: Do you want to go to the Century Fashions sale on Saturday?
B: I'd like to, but the salespeople there are not very professional.
A: I know what you mean. They're not very friendly, either.
B: Yeah, and some of the clothes are nice, but some of them are really bad quality.
A: That's true. I bought a sweater there last winter, and it fell apart after I wore it twice.
B: Also, it takes hours to pay for things. The lines are always really long.
A: Then again, I did get my favorite jeans there!

Unit 4: Apologies and Excuses

page 14, CD 1–17
Listening 1

1.
A: Oh, I'm so sorry. I didn't mean to hit you.
B: Don't worry about it. It's just a little scratch.
A: Here, let me give you my insurance information.
B: That's okay. It's a really old car. It has dozens of dents and scratches already.

2.
A: So, what did you do this weekend, Carrie?
B: Well, I went out to dinner at Sabrina's with my family on Saturday night.
A: Wow, Sabrina's! It's such a nice restaurant. What was the occasion?
B: Um, it was my birthday.
A: Oh, no! Did I forget again this year? I feel terrible. It won't happen again.
B: That's all right. I always forget people's birthdays.

3.
A: Hi, Gina. I don't want to bother you. I just came by to see if you're finished with that CD I loaned you.
B: Oh, sure. Come on in, and I'll get it… Let's see, I had it in my book bag… Uh-oh.

A: Is something wrong?
B: I can't find it. I must have lost it this morning. I'm sorry.
A: Oh, well, that's all right.
B: I'll go buy you a new copy right now.

4.
A: Hi, Sarah. What's wrong? Are you upset?
B: It's 6:30. You were supposed to be here half an hour ago.
A: I'm sorry. There was so much traffic on the freeway. It won't happen again.
B: Well, I'll let it go this time. But you should really leave your house earlier when you have to drive somewhere during rush hour.

5.
A: Oh! Are you okay, Sam?
B: I'm not sure. My ankle hurts a little.
A: I really apologize. I was walking too fast, and I wasn't watching where I was going. I didn't mean to trip you.
B: I know you didn't, but I think my ankle might be sprained.
A: Oh, no. Here, let me help you up. We should go to the hospital.

6.
A: Where were you last night?
B: I was home studying. Why?
A: You were supposed to meet me at the movies last night.
B: Oh, no! I forgot! I'm sorry.
A: I tried to call you, but I kept getting your voicemail.
B: I'm so sorry. Unfortunately, I lost my phone yesterday.

page 15, CD 1–18
Listening 2

1.
A: Hi, Linda. I'm so sorry I'm late.
B: You're really late. You were supposed to be here over an hour ago. What happened?
A: There was heavy traffic on the freeway, and I couldn't call because my cell phone died.
B: That's weird. There isn't usually any traffic at this time of day.
A: I know, but there was a really bad accident on the freeway about ten miles north of here. Traffic was completely stopped for over an hour.
B: Hmm…That's very unusual.

2.
A: Hi, Mike.
B: Hi, Kylie. What's wrong?
A: I have to apologize. I wasn't able to finish my half of our class project last night.
B: But it's due today.
A: I know. I feel terrible about it.
B: What happened?
A: My roommate burned her hand while she was cooking last night, and I had to take her to the emergency room. We were there all night.

B: No wonder you look so tired. Is she okay?
A: Her hand is burned pretty badly, but she'll be all right.

3.
A: Hey, Ken. Why didn't you come to Alex's party last night? We were all expecting to see you there.
B: Oh, I'm sorry about that. I got lost trying to find Alex's house.
A: Really? But I gave you directions.
B: Well, I wrote the directions down wrong.
A: Well, why didn't you call or use the GPS on your phone?
B: Uh, I didn't have my cell phone with me.
A: That's strange. You always carry your cell phone with you.

4.
A: Where have you been? We've been waiting for you. The meeting was supposed to start half an hour ago.
B: I know. I apologize. My car broke down, and I had to wait for a tow truck.
A: Again? Didn't your car break down last week, too?
B: Um, yeah, it did. It's a really old car.
A: And the week before that, you were late because you were helping someone look for their lost cat.
B: I'm sorry. I promise I'll be on time for next week's meeting.

page 16, CD 1–19
Listening 3

1.
A: Tell me all about how it went!
B: I wish I could, but I missed it. I got really sick on Friday night. I thought I had the flu, but it turned out to be food poisoning. I was sick all day Saturday, so I couldn't go to the wedding. I thought my cousin would be mad, but she just felt bad that I was sick all day.

2.
A: Hi, it's Paul. I missed class yesterday. Can you tell me what the homework was?
B: Oh, sorry, I wasn't there yesterday, either. I was on my way to catch the bus when I fell and broke my ankle. One of my neighbors who was on his way to work drove me to the hospital. I'll call Katie and ask her about the homework, and then I'll call you back.

3.
A: How did your sister do yesterday?
B: Well, her team won, but I didn't get to see it! I had just gotten to the soccer field when my boss called. One of my coworkers called in sick with the flu, so he asked me to come in and work.

4.
A: Well, how did it go on Monday?
B: You're not going to believe this, but I missed it! I left really early so I wouldn't be late, but I wrote the address down wrong, and I couldn't find the office. I was so nervous about the interview that I forgot my phone, too, so I couldn't call them and ask for directions. I was so mad at myself. I really wanted that job!

5.
A: So how was it?
B: I don't know because I missed it! I was so disappointed, and so was my niece. I had flowers and a card to give her, and I really wanted to be there for her special day. But I ran out of gas on my way to the school. Can you believe that? I made it to her graduation party later that evening, but I really wanted to make it to the ceremony.

6.
A: So was it fun?
B: Well, I think the people who went had fun, but I had to study for my history test. My friend Kelly went, and she said it was a great party. I hope Sarah has another one for her birthday next year.

page 17, CD 1-20
Pronunciation

1. Is everything okay?
2. Where were you last night?
3. Did you forget our appointment?
4. Why are you so late?

page 17, CD 1-21
Dictation

A: Where were you this afternoon? You were supposed to meet me for lunch.
B: I'm so sorry. I was at a doctor's appointment. I thought I would be out of there by noon, but the appointment took a long time.
A: Oh, are you okay?
B: I'm fine. It was just a check-up. Did you get the movie tickets for tonight?
A: No, I didn't. I'm sorry. I couldn't get online at home.
B: Is something wrong with your Internet connection?
A: I think so. Sometimes I can't get a connection.

Unit 5: Character Traits

page 18, CD 1-22
Listening 1

1.
A: Jeff is the perfect elementary school teacher. He's so good with children.
B: I know what you mean. He never gets angry with those kids, even when they're not listening to him.

2.
A: Sheila speaks very well. When she talks, people stop and listen.
B: I know. A lot of people even change their opinions after talking to her.

3.
A: How does Mary like her new job?
B: Oh, she loves it. She's really excited about working there. In fact, she even works on weekends because she enjoys being there so much.

4.
A: I've been having problems with my boss lately.
B: Why is that?
A: Well, he has a lot of rules. He gets really angry if I come to work two minutes late, or if I let the office phone ring more than twice before I answer it. And if I make a tiny mistake, he yells at me.

5.
A: I don't know about you, but I'm voting for Dave Thomas for school president. He knows everything about this school and all the important issues.
B: Yeah. He really knows what he's talking about.

6.
A: My landlady is really nice. She doesn't get angry if I pay the rent a few days late. And when I'm sick, she always brings me homemade chicken soup.
B: Wow. She sounds really thoughtful.

page 19, CD 1-23
Listening 2

1.
A: What do you think of Chris?
B: I like talking to him. He knows something interesting about practically everything.
A: Yeah, I know. And he's really serious about studying, too. He wants to go to medical school, so his grades have to be perfect.
B: He must be a good student.
A: He's a great student—top of the class last year.

2.
A: You know Brandon Kent, don't you?
B: Oh, sure. He's a really nice guy. He took a whole day off last month to help me move into my new apartment. Then he drove me to the mall so I could pick up some furniture for my new place.
A: Yeah, that's what I like about him. In fact, he's coming over this afternoon to help me with my math assignment.
B: Lucky you!

3.
A: I can't stand that Terry Dey.
B: Really?
A: Yeah. The other day, we were walking down the street past this homeless man who asked us for money. His clothes were torn and dirty.
B: Yeah?
A: Well, as soon as we walked past him, Terry made jokes about his clothes.
B: No way! That's terrible.

4.
A: Are you going to Tony's party on Friday night?
B: Yeah. Are you?
A: Of course. He has great parties, don't you think?
B: Definitely. It's because he gets so excited about everything. Everyone sees him laughing and having fun, and then they start enjoying themselves, too.
A: You're right. He's an amazing guy.

5.
A: Have you seen Patrick recently?
B: No, I haven't. We were supposed to go to a concert last weekend, but he said he was too sick to go.
A: Oh, that's too bad.
B: The thing is, he didn't tell me the truth. My brother saw him at a party the same night, having a good time.
A: Oh! I really hate it when people lie like that.
B: Me, too.

6.
A: I just talked to Chuck.
B: How is he today?
A: The same as usual. He's always in a bad mood. Talking to him is really difficult. It's easy to say something that really upsets him.
B: I know. I wonder why he's like that.
A: I think it's because he isn't doing well at school this year.

page 20, CD 1-24
Listening 3

1.
Now that John has that new job, you wouldn't recognize him. I guess you have to be more conservative when you have a job like that. He works really long hours now and wears a suit and tie. And when he comes home from work, he never wants to go out. All he does is sit in his chair and watch TV. He looks totally exhausted. That's not how he was in college. Back then he used to go around in old T-shirts and jeans. And he had that crazy green hair!

2.
I ran into Akiko the other day. I hardly recognized her. Do you remember her from high school? She was a little chubby and out of shape back then. I don't think she ever exercised or played any sports. Well, she looks really different now. She's lost a lot of weight. In fact, she looks terrific. She told me that she

decided to get in better shape after she got married last year. Now she goes to the gym three times a week.

3.
Have you had a chance to talk to Maria lately? She's gotten so depressed—you know, sad and worried all the time. It's a real change. She used to be so enthusiastic and happy in high school. She was a cheerleader, and she was always laughing and making jokes. Now she just sits in coffee shops all by herself and just looks really sad. You can tell that something is really bothering her. It must be because she and her boyfriend recently broke up.

4.
Do you remember what Ted Rodgers used to look like? He used to be so athletic, with really big muscles. He went to the gym all the time and was always careful about what he ate and drank. Well, you wouldn't believe how much he's changed. I'm sure he weighs over 200 pounds now. It doesn't look like he does any exercise at all, and he eats just about anything. Someone told me he changed after he got really wealthy from Internet stocks. They said that after he got rich, he decided just to enjoy himself.

page 21, CD 1-25
Pronunciation

1. Lee is really caring.
2. He asks a lot of questions.
3. Is she enthusiastic?
4. It's important to be informed.
5. She always does nice things for people.
6. Did he ever call you?

page 21, CD 1-26
Dictation

A: So, tell me about your new neighbor.
B: He's really funny and nice. And we found out we have a lot in common.
A: Oh, really? Like what?
B: Well, he's about the same age as I am. And he used to live in the same neighborhood as I did in New York.
A: Wow! What kinds of things does he like to do?
B: He told me that he always plays soccer on Saturdays. And he likes to go hiking and bike riding. And he loves movies.

Unit 6: Travel

page 22, CD 1-27
Listening 1

1.
Ladies and gentlemen, we hope you enjoyed your flight to Toronto. When we land, you can locate your bags on Carousel 5 in Baggage Claim. Just stay to your left, go down the steps, and Carousel 5 will be on the right past Johnnie's Hamburger Stand.

2.
Passengers on Flight 87 to Miami, your departure gate has been changed to Gate 64. Again, that's Gate 64. You need to take a right past the restaurants and the gift shop to find Gate 64. Passengers on Flight 102 to Tampa, your departure gate is still Gate 62.

3.
Ladies and gentlemen, our crew will be serving refreshments. We'll have complementary soft drinks, juices, and coffee. If you are interested, you may purchase snacks like chips, cookies, or pretzels for three dollars a bag.

4.
Passengers waiting for Flight 774 to Chicago, may I have your attention, please. Your flight will be departing at 11:30. Will passengers Tom and Carrie Simpson please report to an agent as soon as possible at Gate 16?

5.
The 9:20 train to Los Angeles will be departing from Platform 10 in two minutes. All passengers who are waiting for the 9:20 train, will you please proceed to Platform 10 immediately?

6.
Your attention, please. The 12:10 train to Concord has been delayed. The train will now arrive on the same platform at 12:30. That's half past 12:00.

page 23, CD 1-28
Listening 2

1.
Could you please tell me which platform the train to Toronto leaves from? And is it on the right or the left?

2.
Would you please help me get my bags down so I can get off the plane? They're too high for me to reach.

3.
Excuse me, sir. Do you know where the Transamerica Airlines counter is? Is it past the Northern Airlines counter?

4.
Molly, we're about to land, so you need to fasten your seatbelt now. Do you need me to help you?

5.
Let's find window seats so we can see things as they go by. I don't like having to look around other people.

6.
But I have to be in Toronto tonight! Isn't there another flight I could take? I really have to get there tonight!

page 24, CD 1-29
Listening 3

1.
A: How was your flight?
B: Oh, it was great! My flight was overbooked, and the airline asked for volunteers to go on a later flight. I volunteered because the next flight was only an hour later, and the airline gave me $300! It pays to be bumped!

2.
A: Did you have a good flight?
B: Ugh, no, it was terrible.
A: Oh, no! Why?
B: The flight was fully booked, so every seat was taken. I was crammed between this guy who was snoring the whole time and a really messy kid who got his chips all over me. I couldn't wait for it to be over!

3.
A: Did you have any trouble finding the house?
B: No, not at all. We used the GPS. But it sure was a long drive.
A: Did you stop anywhere?
B: Yeah, we stopped at a rest stop about halfway here to get a cold drink and stretch our legs. It was really hot out, and there were a ton of people there. I guess it was a good weekend for road trips.

4.
A: How was the drive?
B: It was okay.
A: Really? You look worn out.
B: Well, I guess we are pretty exhausted. It was so hot out, and the air conditioning broke an hour into the trip. We stopped at the halfway mark to switch drivers and eat lunch. Then we had trouble starting the car.

5.
A: Did you enjoy the ride?
B: Oh, it was great! It was nice to just relax and not have to worry about driving. I read my book and did sudoku puzzles the whole way. And I met some really nice people, too. They were on their way to Boston, too.
I don't know why I've never taken the train before!

6.
A: How was the trip?
B: Pretty good, I guess. I don't really know because I was asleep the whole time.
A: Really?
B: Yeah, pretty much. I started reading a book, but then I fell asleep and didn't wake up until ten minutes after my stop. I had to get off the train and get on another one going the other direction. I'll have to set the alarm on my phone next time.

page 25, CD 1-30
Pronunciation
1. Did you go to Los Angeles?
2. You need to go on vacation.
3. We like to travel.
4. Let's go to Tokyo.
5. It's hard to drive ten hours.
6. I'm going to London.

page 25, CD 1-31
Dictation
A: Welcome back! Tell me about your trip!
B: Oh, it was so much fun! First, we went to New York.
A: Did you go to the Museum of Modern Art?
B: Yes, we loved it. I had always wanted to see that museum. We also went to Central Park, of course, and lots of other sites.
A: Where did you go after that?
B: After New York, we went to Philadelphia for three days. And then we went to Boston for two days. It was a great vacation!

Unit 7: Housing

page 26, CD 1-32
Listening 1
1.
Well, I'm single and I spend a lot of time traveling, so I'm not home very much. So there's really no point in my spending money on a large place with lots of rooms.

2.
We've got three small children, and they like to play outside, so I don't think it makes sense for us to live in a high-rise building.

3.
I work right in the city and I don't have a car. I'd like a place close to my work so that I don't have to spend a lot of time commuting.

4.
I run my own business and I work out of my home. I'm lucky because I don't have to go into town very often, so I'd like a place that's quiet and away from the city.

5.
I need a new place. I need a good-sized apartment because I have two teenage sons, and they each need to have their own bedroom. We want to live downtown, too.

6.
Both my wife and I work for an airline and we'd like something fairly close to work. We don't mind if it's small, because there's only the two of us. We don't even mind the noise of the planes. In fact, we kind of like it.

page 27, CD 1-33
Listening 2
1.
My neighbors are fantastic. They're really friendly, and some of them have great parties, too. I'd like more space, though. There's hardly enough space for all my stuff. I guess I should throw some of it out, but I just can't.

2.
The apartment I rent is okay. It's near a lot of stores, so it's convenient for shopping. The problem, though, is that the owner hasn't spent any money on the place in years. The furniture is falling apart, and the carpet in the living room is stained in places.

3.
There are advantages and disadvantages to living out here in the suburbs. It's not really the most convenient place to live.
It takes forever to get into town, especially during rush hour. And there aren't any good stores out here. On the other hand, it's nice and quiet on the weekends.

4.
I love my apartment. I wish I could afford to stay here. The location is perfect. It has huge windows with a beautiful view, and I love being able to step outside and walk to cafes and shops. The only problem is the rent. It's just too high now, so I can't stay.

5.
My place is huge. It has room for all my stuff, and there's a big kitchen, too. Of course, it's really old, so it needs a coat of paint and some new appliances. The refrigerator and dishwasher are really ancient. And I think the stove is about a hundred years old!

6.
I recently moved into an apartment building for the first time. I've always lived in houses. It takes a while to get used to having neighbors right next door. I feel like they're always listening to me, like they want to know everything I do. It's annoying. But the rent is much cheaper than my old place, and I like that.

page 28, CD 1-34
Listening 3
1.
We used to have a nice apartment downtown. It had great views of the city! But then these new people moved in upstairs. They played loud music all the time, and the sound came straight through the ceiling and into our apartment. It was terrible, so we moved. Now we're living in a nice small house in the suburbs. And our neighbors are very quiet.

2.
My new apartment is on a high floor, and it's great. There's no noise at all. I only hear the birds in the park. Before that, I lived in a first-floor apartment. It had a little yard, which was nice, but I heard people coming and going all the time. And it was close to the street, so I heard all the traffic too.

3.
We didn't really want to move because we loved our apartment. We had a wonderful landlady, too. She didn't raise the rent for years, and if anything was broken, she would get it fixed really fast. But with the children getting older, we needed to be closer to a good school. So that's why we moved. Now we live in an apartment in the suburbs.

4.
I used to live in a nice apartment downtown, in a pretty interesting neighborhood. But the thing was, they wouldn't let you keep a pet. I really wanted to get a cat, so I moved to a place where you could keep pets. Now I live in a building near the park. And there's two of us—me and my cat, Felix. We play all the time.

5.
My new apartment has a huge kitchen and a great stove. I'm really happy about it. I love to cook and have parties, but the kitchen in my old place was *so* tiny. And the dining room was small, too. The location was good, but I could never have people over for dinner, so I needed to find something different.

6.
I used to live in a house. I had a nice yard in the front, and another yard in the back. The trouble was the maintenance. It was really expensive to take care of. So I moved. Now I live in an apartment with no yard. Even though I have much less space now, it's wonderful, because it's a lot cheaper.

page 29, CD 1-35
Pronunciation
1. My apartment building is five stories high.
2. My sons are in college.
3. The yard is pretty big.
4. Our neighbors are very quiet.
5. My house is too small for my family.
6. The bathrooms are small.

page 29, CD 1-36
Dictation
A: How's it going? Do you like your new apartment?
B: Oh, I love it. My neighbors are really friendly, and the landlord is nice.
A: That's great! What's the building like?
B: The building is ten stories high, and

there are ten apartments on each floor. So, I guess there are 100 apartments.
A: Wow, it sounds huge. Have you seen some of the other apartments?
B: Yeah, my next-door neighbor invited me over for coffee the other day. She and her husband are doctors. They've been in the building for five years.

Unit 8: Can You Believe It?

page 30, CD 1–37
Listening 1

1.
A: Did you hear about that woman in Florida?
B: No, what happened?
A: She pulled out the power cable to her office building so she could be sent home early with pay.
B: No way!
A: Yeah, and she had done the same thing to the telephone lines in the past in order to get out of work.
B: That's awful! What finally happened to her?
A: She lost her job and was arrested for damaging property.

2.
A: Did you hear about the woman who has to spend a month in jail because her pet is too overweight?
B: What? No!
A: Yeah, her pot-bellied pig weighs 200 pounds. Most weigh between 65 and 100 pounds. It's unhealthy for the poor animal to be that big, and it has trouble walking.
B: So what happened?
A: Well, the police charged her with animal neglect. She also has to pay a $500 fine.

3.
A: What are you laughing about?
B: This story I'm reading. You know how call-forwarding works, right?
A: Yeah, you can have calls to one phone number forwarded to another number.
B: Right. Well, this plumber in Pennsylvania had the calls to five other plumbers forwarded to his own business.
A: So he stole the other plumbers' customers?
B: Yeah, but just the customers with big expensive jobs. He's in jail now, and lost his plumber's license.

4.
A: I just read something amazing in the news.
B: What was it?
A: These two robbers robbed a convenience store.
B: What happened next?

A: Well, after the robbery, they decided to steal a car.
B: Yeah? Did they get away?
A: No. They jumped in the stolen getaway car, but couldn't drive it!
B: Why was that?
A: Because the guy didn't know how to drive a car with a stick shift! And so the police caught them!

5.
A: Did you read this story about the man in Sweden?
B: No, what happened?
A: It says, "Customs officials in Sweden had an unusual experience today. As a man was going through the customs checkpoint, officers noticed that his shirt was moving."
B: That's weird.
A: Yeah, I know. Listen. "When they searched him, they found 65 baby snakes and six lizards inside his shirt. The man said he wanted to open a reptile farm. They arrested him for smuggling."

6.
A: Did you hear about that guy who tried to rob a pharmacy in Canada?
B: No, what happened?
A: He was in the drugstore, and he told the employees there that he was going to come back in half an hour and rob them.
B: So what did they do?
A: They called the police, of course. So when the guy came back 30 minutes later with his friend, the police were waiting for them.
B: Oh, that's hilarious!

page 31, CD 1–38
Listening 2

1.
A young man in Illinois was having trouble paying his college tuition, so he came up with quite a creative solution. He wrote to a newspaper columnist and asked him to print a request in his column. He wanted the columnist to ask readers to send in one penny to help him pay for his college education. Readers of the newspaper thought it was a funny idea, so they sent in their pennies, and in the end, the young man collected $28,000.

2.
An American football team wants to hire 250 students to help them get their new football arena ready for visitors. The job? Flushing toilets. Apparently, when a new stadium or arena is built, you have to make sure all the plumbing is working properly before you can open for business. And the only way to do that is to flush all the toilets at the same time.

3.
We all know that Egyptians mummified their pharaohs when they died in order to preserve their bodies for eternity. The Egyptians had an elaborate process for mummification involving various chemicals and techniques. But they may have been better off just going to Colombia, South America. It's been discovered that the soil in the town of San Bernardo, Colombia contains ingredients that naturally mummify anyone buried there.

4.
What would you do if you were bored with your job because you didn't have enough work to do? Would you quit? That's not what a man working in a New Mexico government office did. Instead, he decided to sue his employer for "wrongful hiring." He argues that he left a higher-paying business job to take the government job and ended up with nothing to do!

page 32, CD 1–39
Listening 3

1.
A: Hey, listen to this. "In Florida today, a man was found drifting about a mile offshore. He was on a swimming pool float sound asleep." Can you believe that?
B: No way! What was he doing out there?
A: Let's see… It says, "Apparently, the man had fallen asleep and wasn't aware that he was drifting out to sea. After rescuing him, the Coast Guard said that he was very lucky that they found him."

2.
A: Wow, did you hear about the twin sisters that were separated at birth?
B: No, what happened?
A: They were adopted by different families when they were babies and grew up in different cities.
B: Yeah?
A: But after high school, they both attended the same college!
B: Wow! And they met there?
A: Yes! They figured out they were twins. They were even in the same class!

3.
A: Hey, has an airline ever lost your luggage?
B: Yeah, once.
A: Well, this British guy claimed that different airlines lost his luggage dozens of times. And since the airlines pay you when they lose your luggage, he's gotten about $135,000 in lost luggage claims.
B: Wow, that's amazing.
A: It sounds amazing, but it isn't really. The guy had an illegal scam going. He would check two or three bags. Then when he reached his destination, he would put one bag inside another one and claim that it was lost!

4.

A: I just read the most amazing story online.
B: What was it about?
A: Well, this guy in Florida found a camera floating in the ocean in a plastic case. He decided he would try to find the owner of the camera, so he posted the photos online. Believe it or not, people who saw the photos helped him identify the owner of the camera. And it turns out the owner had dropped it in the ocean in Aruba several months earlier! It had floated 1,000 miles!

5.

A: Did you hear that amazing story about the newborn twins?
B: Yeah, one twin was really sick, right?
A: That's right. She wouldn't stop crying, and she was turning blue. No one could calm her. Then a nurse at the hospital put her twin sister next to her, and when the healthy twin put her arm over her sister, the sick twin stopped crying and started getting better!

6.

A: Wow, I think I need to get a parrot!
B: Why? What are you reading about?
A: I'm reading a story about a parrot that saved two people's lives. A man and his son fell asleep on the couch watching a movie. While they were sleeping, their house caught on fire. They woke up suddenly when they heard their parrot imitating a smoke alarm. Apparently, their smoke alarm did go off, but it wasn't loud enough to wake them up.

page 33, CD 1–40
Pronunciation

1. The drugstore employees called the police after he left.
2. When he came back, the police were waiting for him.
3. While they were sleeping, their house caught on fire.
4. The smoke alarm went off, but it didn't wake them up.

page 33, CD 1–41
Dictation

A: Did you hear about that guy who sent himself somewhere in a box?
B: What? No! What happened?
A: Well, this guy wanted to go to Dallas to visit his father, but he didn't want to pay for a plane ticket.
B: Yeah? What did he do?
A: He figured he would save money by mailing himself to Dallas, so he packed himself inside a box!
B: You're kidding me! That must have been some trip!

Unit 9: Friendship

page 34, CD 2–2
Listening 1

1.
I really like Allison. She's such fun to be with. She always makes me laugh. Did she tell you the story about her first day of school? I don't think I've laughed so hard in my whole life!

2.
I went out with this guy a couple of times, Ted Roberts. Maybe you know him. He's okay, I guess, but the guy's got no future. I think he just wants to spend the rest of his life surfing at the beach.

3.
Tony Lee asked me out the other night, and I said no. You know, he is really embarrassing to be with. Last time I went out to a party with him, he nearly got into a fight with someone. And then he wouldn't leave the party, even after everyone else left.

4.
I've been out with Sandra Bronstein twice. She's really an interesting person. I didn't realize her father is a pretty well-known artist and her mother is a successful stockbroker. I'd really like to meet her parents sometime.

5.
Do you know Rod, the guy in our Spanish class? Anyway, he's invited me out on a date. You know the guy I mean—he's kind of thin, very tall, with long curly hair. And he's got those dark brown eyes. Just my type!

6.
I was stuck sitting next to Martha at a dinner party the other evening. No matter what I said or did, I couldn't get her to laugh. I wonder why she is so terribly serious.

page 35, CD 2–3
Listening 2

1.
A: Hello.
B: Oh, hello, Lance. This is Dave.
A: Oh, hi! How are you?
B: Fine, thanks. Hey, are you doing anything on Saturday?
A: Not really.
B: Well, some friends of mine are having a barbecue. Do you want to come with me?
A: Oh, that sounds like fun. What can I bring?

2.
A: Hello.
B: Hey, Paula. It's Tina. I'm calling about next week. I wondered if you had anything planned for Wednesday.
A: No, not really. Why?
B: Well, there's going to be a talk at the bookstore, by that guy whose book we read in class last semester. Remember?
A: Oh, yeah. Sure. That sounds kind of interesting, and I don't really have plans.
B: Great! I'll meet you at the bookstore Wednesday at 7.

3.
A: Hi, Rose. How are you?
B: Not bad. And you?
A: Okay. Listen, are you interested in going to an art show on Sunday? A friend of mine is having an exhibition of her paintings. It's the opening night—free drinks and food.
B: Well, actually, I don't have anything planned. It sounds kind of fun. Why not?
A: Well then, why don't I pick you up at 6:30?
B. Okay. I'll be ready and waiting.

4.
A: Hi, Melissa.
B: Oh, hello, Suzie.
A: Do you have any plans for tonight? A few friends and I were thinking of going out for a pizza.
B: Gee, I'd really love to. But I have to work late.
A: Oh, that's too bad.
B: Yeah. I really wish I could go.

5.
A: Doing anything after class?
B: Nothing much.
A: Why don't we go downtown and take a look at the new shoe store?
B: Great idea. I need some new gym shoes.
A: I don't really need new shoes. I just love shoe shopping!
B: See you after class then.

6.
A: Hey, George, are you interested in going to the car show? It's going on at the exhibition center.
B: Yeah, I like those kinds of shows. When is it?
A: It opens on Saturday morning.
B: How about we go in the afternoon? I want to sleep late.
A: That's fine with me.

page 36, CD 2–4
Listening 3

1.
A: I'd really like to see this. Kids from all over the country are participating. And the things they're playing sound really

difficult. There's one kid who's been playing the violin since he was two years old!
B: When is it?
A: Let's see…It's Saturday afternoon.
B: I'd really like to see it, but I was planning to watch soccer on TV that day.

2.
A: Hey, this sounds interesting. You get to see how all sorts of unusual foods are prepared, and you get to try different dishes, too. They have chefs from Japan and India, from China, from Mexico, and from Italy, too. What do you think?
B: Well, it does sound interesting, but I can't. I've just started a new diet, so I can't eat too much.

3.
A: Let's go and see this. I love these kinds of events. A lot of famous people are going to be there. All of the actors who are in it are coming to see it, and the director and producer are going to be there, too.
B: Really?
A: Yeah. We'd need to get to the theater early, though, to get a good view. Thousands of people always show up for these premieres.
B: Actually, I'd rather not go. I don't like big crowds.

4.
A: This event down at the bookstore could be interesting. It'll be a chance to get a famous person's autograph.
B: Oh, yeah? Are you into autographs?
A: Sure. It's fun to meet famous people.
B: Yeah, but she's not really one of my favorite writers. In fact, I think her books are kind of boring.

5.
A: Let's go and watch this tomorrow afternoon. It should be a good game. The home team just got two new really good players.
B: But haven't they lost a lot of games recently?
A: Well, yeah. But they're playing better now.
B: Thanks for asking me, but I think I'll stay home. I heard it's going to be pretty cold tomorrow.

6.
A: Let's check out this exhibition at the gallery downtown. The artists seem pretty talented.
B: Hmm. What artists? Any big names?
A: No, not really. They're all local artists.
B: Well, thanks anyway, but I'm only interested in seeing works by famous artists.

page 37, CD 2-5
Pronunciation
1. She's such fun to be with.
2. She's really an interesting person.
3. She's the only teacher I really like.
4. He is really embarrassing to be with.
5. He's kind of thin and very tall.
6. I just love his sense of humor.

page 37, CD 2-6
Dictation
A: Do you know Sandra Thomas?
B: Yeah, I do. Why do you ask?
A: She's in my history class. I really like her. She's so funny.
B: I know. She makes me laugh all the time.
A: She seems very intelligent, too.
B: She really is smart. She gets As in all her classes. Have you met her brother and sister?
A: No, what are they like? Are they like Sandra?
B: Her brother's completely different. He's intelligent, but he's not friendly at all.

Unit 10: Television

page 38, CD 2-7
Listening 1
1.
A: Did you watch it today? I missed it.
B: It was great. One of the best episodes ever! Ted married Isabella, and Isabella's daughter is upset. So now Ted's worried, and Isabella's miserable. I can't wait to see what happens tomorrow.

2.
A: Did you watch the show last night?
B: I started to, but I had to go out. Did you see it?
A: Yeah.
B: Who won the grand prize?
A: A 20-year-old university student. She won a new car.

3.
A: How was that show you watched the other night?
B: It was crazy! All the people on the show were constantly arguing and saying mean things about each other. I don't know why anyone would want to be on a show like that.
A: I know, me neither. Are you going to watch it again?
B: Definitely. I want to see if Erica and Lisa get in another fight!

4.
A: Did you hear about what happened in Florida?
B: No, what happened?

A: Well, there was a huge hurricane there yesterday.
B: Really. That's terrible!
A: I know! And there were some major floods. Lots of people have had to move out of their homes.

5.
A: Did you watch the game?
B: Yeah, it was pretty exciting. Too bad our team lost, though.
A: Yeah, I thought they were going to win this time.
B: I know. But they really need to work on their defense.

6.
A: Did you like that show you were watching when I called last night?
B: Yeah, I thought it was pretty interesting. I always wonder how they can take video of birds flying like that. You get the impression you're up there flying with them.

page 39, CD 2-8
Listening 2
1.
At 9:30 p.m. tonight, a panel of experts will discuss developments in information technology and how new innovations are going to change the way we watch TV. If you like to know about the latest trends in technology, this is the show for you.

2.
At 10 o'clock. we'll present a documentary about new treatments for cancer. It will report on major breakthroughs in cancer research, including an exciting new treatment for skin cancer and information about cancer-fighting foods that you probably have in your kitchen right now. If you have cancer or know someone who does, please don't miss this program.

3.
At 10:30, learn about modern architecture and the influence that some of the major 20th century architects had on cities around the world.

4.
Coming up on AFC tonight is *Sea Crazy*, a new sitcom about a cruise ship where everything goes wrong. Tonight, the kitchen staff goes on strike, and the passengers have to cook their own meals—with hilarious results. If you're thinking about taking a cruise, stay tuned for this one.

5.
Tonight at 10 p.m., only on AFC, watch the final round of the game show *Question Time*. Twenty contestants will play for the big prize—one million dollars! They'll answer questions about history, movies, sports, and even math. If you love facts and trivia, this is the show for you.

6.
Later tonight, it's America's number one late night talk show, *The Night Show*. Tonight's guests are movie star Stephanie Sanchez and rapper B Cash B.

page 40, CD 2-9
Listening 3

1.
A: Oh, that cooking show I like is on tonight. I love the chef on that program.
B: Yeah. She's that British chef, right? I really like her, too. I've tried some of her recipes. They were really good, and none of them were that difficult to make.

2.
A: Hey, Liz, do you watch that reality show, *Who Wants to Marry Me?* The finale is on tonight!
B: Well, honestly, I think those shows are really frustrating to watch. The people on those shows fight all the time.
A: Oh, I love watching them argue with each other! But I guess you don't want to watch it with me.
B: No. Sorry.

3.
A: Are you going to watch the tennis match on Saturday afternoon? It looks like it's going to be a good one.
B: I know, but I don't really enjoy watching tennis on TV. I'd rather play tennis than watch it.

4.
A: Hey, there's an interesting documentary about space travel on TV tomorrow. Let's watch it.
B: Okay. I love science documentaries. You learn so much more from them than you ever learn in school.

5.
A: Hey, that travel show is on tonight. You know the one—they follow this guy on his vacation, and he always tries to find the cheapest places to stay. Sometimes the places are dirty and full of bugs. It's fun to watch.
B: Actually, that doesn't sound very interesting to me. I'd rather watch a show about staying at expensive hotels!

6.
A: Oh, that antiques show is on tonight.
B: I love that show. People bring their antique furniture and stuff. Sometimes their old junk turns out to be worth thousands of dollars. It's really amazing.
A: I think it's kind of boring. I'd rather watch something exciting, like an action movie—or sports.

page 41, CD 2-10
Pronunciation

1. It was great.
2. It was terrible!
3. It was one of the best episodes ever!
4. I thought it was boring.

CD 2-11
1. I thought it was pretty interesting.
2. It was really frustrating to watch.
3. That novel was truly amazing!
4. That new movie was frightening.

page 41, CD 2-12
Dictation

A: How did you like that new show that was on Wednesday night?
B: Oh, I thought it was really exciting! I can't wait to find out why those people are on the island. What did you think?
A: I didn't think it was interesting at all. I was bored.
B: Really? You thought it was boring? But there was so much drama and excitement!
A: I think shows like that are frustrating to watch. You never know what's going on.
B: Oh, that's exactly why I think they're so fun to watch. I can't wait for next week's show!

Unit 11: Cities

page 42, CD 2-13
Listening 1

1.
When I went to Hawaii, I spent the first few days in Honolulu. Everything was really expensive there, especially in the restaurants. Four dollars for a soda! But the beaches were wonderful. The sand was so soft and the water was so clean.

2.
Sydney is one of my favorite cities in Australia. There are some great buildings there, like the famous opera house. The only problem is the weather. Spring and fall are okay, but the summer is too hot for me.

3.
Vancouver is a nice city to visit, but don't go in the winter. It's much too cold! The rest of the year is great, though. And there are plenty of clubs, restaurants, and other places to go at night.

4.
One of my favorite cities is New York. There's so much culture there. I spent two weeks there last summer, and every day I went to a different museum, play, musical performance, or poetry reading. The only thing I don't like about New York is the traffic noise. You can hear cars driving and honking all night long.

5.
I think Rio de Janeiro is one of the most interesting cities in South America. The nightlife is great. They have great musicians, so there's always good music in the cafes. Crime is a problem, though, so you have to be careful.

6.
In Los Angeles, you have to drive everywhere, and sometimes the traffic is terrible. But that's the only bad part. There are a lot of fun things to see, like Hollywood, Disneyland, museums, and movie studios.

page 43, CD 2-14
Listening 2

1.
A: Hey, Paul, guess what? I'm going to visit Quebec next summer. I have to go to a friend's wedding, but I also plan to stay a while and do some sightseeing.
B: That's great, Dave, you're going to love it. But do you mean the province of Quebec or Quebec City?
A: I guess I mean the province. The wedding is in Montreal, so I'm going there first. I'll be there for about four days. Montreal is the capital of the province, right?
B: People often think it is because it's the biggest city in the province, but it's not actually the capital. Quebec City is the capital. But Montreal is great. The St. Lawrence River runs right through the middle of the city. It's beautiful in the winter.
A: Wow. And how about the language? My French is okay, but not great. I know most people there speak French, but can I get by with English?
B: Well, people speak both French and English there, but you'll hear French most of the time, and all of the street signs are in French. In fact, Montreal's the third largest French-speaking city in the world. So you'd better practice your French before you go.
A: Okay, I'll do that. Now, what about Quebec City? I'm going to visit a friend from college who lives there now. What's it like?
B: It's a beautiful city. Very old. A lot of the buildings have been nicely restored. Some of them were built in the 17th and 18th centuries. You'll love it there.
A: Great! I can't wait to go!

page 44, CD 2-15
Listening 3

1.
My trip to Cancun this summer was great. The thing I liked most was going

snorkeling at the beach. The water was crystal clear and full of the most beautiful tropical fish I've ever seen. I'll never forget it. Unfortunately, though, I spent too much time in the sun and I got the worst sunburn of my life. I had to go to the doctor to get a cream for it. Next time I go, I'll use sunscreen every day.

2.
You wouldn't believe what happened on my vacation to Bangkok. I lost my wallet in the taxi! I thought I would never see it again. But that evening, the taxi driver came to my hotel and gave my wallet back to me. I was so relieved! The last day I was there, though, I got food poisoning from some fish I had at a restaurant near my hotel. Next time, I'll eat at a different seafood restaurant.

3.
While I was in Athens last summer, I met a really nice Greek family on the boat to the island of Corfu. They invited me to spend a few days with them at their beach house there. What a great house! Anyway, I also went down to Crete. I arrived without a hotel reservation and every place I tried was full, so I had to sleep at the bus station for the first two nights. It was awful. Next time, I'll make reservations before I go.

4.
I went to Mexico City for the first time last summer, and I managed to use my Spanish every day. I mean, I still had to look up words a lot, but I was really proud of myself. The only bad experience I had there was when someone stole my purse while I was having lunch in a restaurant. Next time, I'll watch my purse more carefully.

5.
I really enjoyed my visit to London. I wish I could have stayed there for a month instead of just for a week. The thing I really enjoyed most was the British theater. I went almost every night and saw some really famous actors. Unfortunately, I didn't realize how expensive London can be. I spent twice as much money as I had planned to.

6.
I just came back from a vacation in Tokyo. I did just about everything a person could do there—I even went to Tokyo Disneyland. In fact, I had such a good time there that I went back again the next day. One thing I didn't realize, however, was how cold Tokyo can be in the winter. I didn't take enough warm clothing with me, so I had to buy a coat, a hat, and gloves so I wouldn't freeze.

page 45, CD 2-16
Pronunciation

1. I have to go to a friend's wedding.
2. I had to sleep at the bus station.
3. You've got to go to Rio!
4. Did you have to fly there?

page 45, CD 2-17
Dictation

A: How was your trip to Paris?
B: It was so much fun! But the airline lost my luggage on the way there.
A: Oh no! Did you have to buy new clothes?
B: I had to buy a toothbrush for that night, but they found my suitcase the next day. And they delivered it to my hotel so I didn't have to go pick it up.
A: That's great! Did you rent a car?
B: No, you really don't have to drive there. You can take the Metro everywhere. That's what the subway is called in Paris.

Unit 12: Urban Life

page 46, CD 2-18
Listening 1

1.
It used to take me about an hour to get to the airport, but now it takes me more than two hours. There's so much traffic here these days.

2.
There used to be some really good stores on King Street, but most of them moved to the new mall downtown. Now King Street looks pretty deserted.

3.
The city council has done a great job of providing places for kids to go in their free time. The community center has some great after-school programs now, and there's a new skate park on Market Street.

4.
There didn't use to be a lot of jobs for young people in the city, but there are a lot now. You see lots of companies advertising to train young, inexperienced workers.

5.
I used to eat out a lot, but I don't eat out much anymore. All the good inexpensive places near my apartment have moved or gone out of business. Now there are only really expensive restaurants in my neighborhood. It's really too bad.

6.
They built the new highway over there a couple of years ago. We used to hear the cars and trucks all day and night. But then they planted trees along the side of the road to form a sound barrier. Now it's nice and quiet. And pretty, too.

page 47, CD 2-19
Listening 2

1.
There are hardly any trees downtown now. They cut down a lot of trees when they built the new stores. It's not as green anymore.

2.
My school still looks the same as ever. It hasn't changed at all, except now there's no fence around it. I think it looks nicer without it.

3.
Remember that building with all the windows on King Street? They tore it down and they're going to redevelop the site. It's probably for the best since the building has been empty for so long.

4.
We do all our shopping at the new outdoor farmer's market near our house. There used to be a supermarket there, but it wasn't very good, so some local farmers got together and started the farmer's market. Everyone loves it. In fact, it's very crowded there on the weekends.

5.
There didn't use to be any industry in my hometown. People used to come here to enjoy the beautiful scenery. Now no one comes here because of all the factories and traffic.

6.
The young people in town used to go to a club downtown next to all the office buildings. Now they go to the new skate park. It's better because they're outside, they get some exercise, and have fun!

page 48, CD 2-20
Listening 3

1.
A: I love living here. The best thing is the choice of stores. There are some great bookstores around here, and I love just browsing for an hour or so to see what's on sale.
B: Yeah. That's nice.
A: We do need some better restaurants, though. There are too many fast food places. They should open a place that serves really good salads. I'd love that.
B: So would I.

2.
A: The only thing I don't like about my city is the mall. Everything is too expensive there. They should have a few cheap stores, too.
B: What about downtown? Is there anything to do there?

A: Oh, sure. There are at least a dozen great places to eat downtown. There's Chinese food, sushi, Mexican food, and even a Greek place.
B: Oh, I love Greek food. Let's go there sometime.

3.
A: I think the city council does a great job of keeping the streets clean. There isn't a lot of trash all over the place.
B: That *is* nice.
A: But we could use more green space. They should build a few more parks downtown with lots of trees.
B: That's a good idea.

4.
A: This city is so boring at night. Nothing ever happens. I wish we had some fun clubs to go to.
B: Yeah, me, too.
A: On the other hand, I love that there's almost no crime. You can walk anywhere, even at night, and feel completely safe.
B: You're right about that.

5.
A: The traffic in this city is pretty bad. During rush hour, it can take an hour to drive twenty miles. We need bigger highways.
B: What about the public transportation?
A: It's great, actually. The subway trains are clean and fast, and they run all the time. I just wish I lived near a station!

6.
A: You know what I love about this town? It's such a healthy place to live. There are so many trees, and the air quality is so good. I guess that's because there's not a lot of industry around here.
B: Yeah. You're probably right.
A: But, of course, no industry means no jobs. It can be very difficult to find work around here. The city should try to bring more businesses here.
B: I agree.

page 49, CD 2-21
Pronunciation

1. There didn't use to be a lot of jobs.
2. We used to hear the cars all day and night.
3. The kids used to skateboard in the street.
4. I used to eat out a lot.
5. There used to be a supermarket here.
6. There didn't use to be any industry here.

page 49, CD 2-22
Dictation

A: This city has changed so much in the past five years.
B: What do you mean?

A: Well, there didn't use to be anything for kids to do after school, but now there's a great after-school program at the community center.
B: That's true. There are a lot of fun things for kids to do now.
A: Also, there used to be a lot of crime downtown, and there didn't use to be a lot of good restaurants there.
B: Yeah. It's safe downtown now, and there are lots of great places to eat.

Unit 13: Special Days

page 50, CD 2-23
Listening 1

1.
This special day is always on the third Sunday in June. Families celebrate their dads with gifts like neckties, cologne, or a nice homemade meal.

2.
This special day is usually celebrated on October 5 worldwide. It's to honor and thank teachers for all their hard work, dedication, and contributions to their students and schools.

3.
It's on the second Sunday in May. Most children give their mom flowers or a gift to thank her for all she's done for them. In some families, children bring their mothers breakfast in bed or take her out to dinner.

4.
It's on the evening of December 31st. Lots of people have parties that start late and go on until long after midnight.

5.
This is a day in the spring when adults celebrate kids and spend the day with them. Sometimes the children get special gifts. In some countries kids are given free admission to museums and amusement parks.

6.
This special day is on April 22nd. It celebrates the Earth's natural environment. People get together to plant trees, clean up parks, or create community gardens.

page 51, CD 2-24
Listening 2

1.
My best friend usually takes me out to dinner. We've been doing this since we were in high school, and it's lots of fun. She pays for the meal, but I don't let her buy me a present. Instead, I buy myself a present! That way I always get something I really want.

2.
I usually invite my classmates to go out and party with me. About 10 of us get together. We start out at a restaurant, and then we go downtown. Last year we went to six different clubs in one night. It was wild! It's the one time a year when my parents don't care if I stay out late.

3.
My two children always take me out to a restaurant for dinner. I'm glad they do that instead of spending a lot of money on presents. They're still in school, so they can't afford to buy expensive gifts.

4.
I always celebrated my birthday when I was younger. I'd have a big party and invite everyone I knew. Sometimes I'd have more than 50 people at my place. Those were the days! I don't do anything like that anymore. Since I turned 35, I'd rather not remind myself that I'm a year older. Now I just have a nice dinner at home with my family.

5.
My parents let me invite all my friends over to my house for a party. Usually I have about 25 people over. We always have a lot of fun opening presents, watching videos, and singing along to the radio—stuff like that. My parents are great. They stay upstairs, and they don't bother us.

6.
Well, I always have a quiet birthday at home with my husband, George. He takes over the kitchen for the day and bakes a nice cake for me. I prefer that to going out to a restaurant.

page 52, CD 2-25
Listening 3

1.
I'm a big fan of Valentine's Day. It's one of my favorite days of the year. I love opening and reading those cards and trying to guess who they're from. And last year I got a real valentine, too—you know, from someone who really liked me. That was so romantic.

2.
I don't know why people still play tricks on April Fool's Day. Last year on April first, one of my co-workers played a really horrible trick on our office. He moved all the stuff on everyone's desks around, so no one could find what they were looking for. It was a total waste of time.

3.
Earth Day is really amazing. People spend their time helping each other and nature. Last year, my book club planted flowers around the kids' playground in the park. Then we had a picnic with lots of fresh fruits and vegetables. I hope we do something just as special this year!

4.

When I was a kid, we used to surprise my mom every Mother's Day with breakfast in bed. We got up early and made a mess in the kitchen, but she always enjoyed it. At least I think she did! It was a great tradition and we had fun cleaning up the kitchen together.

5.

Father's Day is a special time for me. It's great because I get to spend the whole day with my family. Last year, our whole family got together for a big dinner. They made my favorite meal, spaghetti and meatballs, and we had ice cream for dessert. We're all big talkers, so everyone had funny stories to tell.

6.

I don't look forward to New Year's Eve. Those parties are the worst. There's way too much food, and you end up eating too much and staying up too late, and you feel terrible the next day. And the noise! Last year, the people next door had a huge, noisy party that went on till five in the morning!

page 53, CD 2–26
Pronunciation

1. Mark is turning twenty-one in September.
2. This will be their fiftieth wedding anniversary!
3. Her birthday is on the thirty-first.

page 53, CD 2–27
Dictation

A: Hey, Alex. What's up?
B: Oh, nothing. I'm just planning for my dad's sixtieth birthday.
A: Wow. Your dad's sixty already? He looks so young. I would have thought he was fifty years old.
B: Ha! He'd love to hear that. Anyway, it's a special occasion, so I want to plan a surprise party for him.
A: That's nice. I'm sure he'll appreciate that. So when's the big day?
B: On the thirtieth.
A: That's only two weeks away! You'd better start planning!

Unit 14: Fashion

page 54, CD 2–28
Listening 1

1.
Oh, this is typical early 60s. That's when guys started to wear their hair a little longer. And girls wore skirts or dresses. I love the wide belts and the boots that girls used to wear.

2.
This must be the 1920s. I love the dresses women wore then—very straight and they came down to just above the knees. And they wore their hair short sometimes with a little wave. Men looked handsome, too, with those wide trousers. They hung out in jazz clubs all the time. What a wild time that was! No wonder they called it the "Roaring Twenties."

3.
This is the late 60s-early 70s, of course. Look at this woman's long tie-dyed skirt. It's so colorful. The guys wore jeans and T-shirts with peace signs on them! And all the young people had long hair back then.

4.
This must be the 1950s, when boys had their hair slicked back and wore high school letterman jackets and tight jeans. I wonder how they ever got into them—or out of them for that matter. The girls wore sweaters, neck scarves, and wide skirts.

5.
Oh, this is the late 70s or early 80s, I think. Both the guy and the girl have punk hairstyles and they're wearing lots of black leather. But it's hard to tell when this is exactly because some people still look this way!

6.
This has to be around 1910. People dressed very formally back then. Men had suits with long jackets and they usually wore black hats. The women wore long dresses and capes. They looked very elegant.

page 55, CD 2–28
Listening 2

1.
A: I just ran into Mary. Wow! She's really changed!
B: Really?
A: Oh, yeah. She used to look really wild. Remember, with all that big hair and makeup? And that leather jacket?
B: Sure. I remember.
A: Well, that's all gone. Now she wears plain, conservative blouses, and her hair is much neater.
B: Weird. Do you know why she changed?
A: Yeah. She just finished college and is looking for a job, so wanted a different look.

2.
A: Beth's dressing differently these days.
B: Oh, really?
A: Yeah. I think it's a change for the better. She used to wear unflattering suits all the time. They were always too big for her.
B: Yeah, I thought the same thing.
A: Now she's wearing fantastic fitted suits in bright colors. My favorite is her red suit.
B: So, why the change?
A: She was on one of those makeover reality shows! They gave her advice on how to dress, and gave her $10,000 to buy new clothes!

3.
A: Have you seen Jake lately?
B: No. Why?
A: Well, he's really changed his look. He used to have that preppy look—you know, the khaki pants and shirts with collars. And short hair.
B: And now?
A: Now he's got long hair, and wears it in a ponytail. And he always wears dark clothes.
B: Interesting. What made him change?
A: He got a new job at an Internet company, and the atmosphere there is really casual. Apparently, everyone wears jeans to work every day.

4.
A: David's really changed the way he looks.
B: Really?
A: Yeah. I never thought I'd see him dressing the way he does now—the blue jeans, the gold necklaces… He's even wearing his shirts unbuttoned.
B: No way!
A: It's true. He used to wear suits and ties all the time, but not anymore.
B: What happened?
A: I heard he broke up with his girlfriend.

5.
A: I think Karen looked a lot better before she changed her look.
B: Hmm. What do you mean?
A: Well, first of all, she cut her gorgeous long hair. And now she dresses completely differently. She used to always look casual but professional. But now she always wears really conservative suits.
B: Why did she change?
A: She had to. She got a big promotion at work, and she meets with clients all the time now.

6.
A: Have you seen Steve Jones since he graduated from college? He looks so different.
B: Really? How?
A: He wears a suit and tie every day.
B: You're kidding!
A: I know. It's strange. In college, he was always wearing his old jeans and a denim shirt. He looked so relaxed all the time.
B: What made him change?
A: He got a job at a bank, so he has to look professional.

page 56, CD 2–30
Listening 3

1.
I just bought these. Do you like them? They're imported from Italy, and they're made of leather. They'll look great with my new pants. They're so comfortable to wear. I walked around in them in the store, so I

know they won't hurt my feet. They were a pretty good bargain, too—only $125.

2.
What do you think of this? Are the arms long enough? I really need it for work. These days we have to dress up at the office, so I can't just wear a shirt and tie. It's made of wool, so it'll be nice and warm in the winter. It was on sale for $75.

3.
This is made of silk, and it was made in China. It's very light, and I love the way it feels. I have to go to a wedding in San Diego this summer. It can get really hot there, so I wanted something sleeveless. I thought it was a bargain at $200.

4.
These will be great for work. They're made of extra-thick denim, and the quality seems good. That's really important to me. I tore a hole in my last pair the first time I wore them. Working in construction is hard on my clothes. I can't believe these were only $29.95!

5.
Does this look okay on me? It's not too tight, is it? It's imported from France and really well-made. I thought the colors were great, and I have a couple of blouses that will go perfectly with it. It's made of wool, too, so it will be very warm. It wasn't cheap—$95—but I know I'll wear it all the time.

6.
These will be great for running. They were pretty expensive—$115. They're imported from Korea and look very well-made. They're really comfortable. And I like these little stripes down the side. I'm going to want to run every day now just so I can wear them!

page 57, CD 2–31
Pronunciation

1. It's made of leather.
2. I need a couple of skirts.
3. She has a lot of suits.
4. He owns lots of T-shirts.
5. It's not made of wool.
6. Can I look at one of those jackets?

page 57, CD 2–32
Dictation

A: Oh, I like this black sweater. It's really nice, isn't it?
B: Yeah, it's great. Is it made of wool?
A: No, I think it's made of cotton.
B: Don't you already have a couple of black sweaters?
A: Yeah, I do, but I really like this one.
B: You wear a lot of black. Why don't you try on one of these blue sweaters?
A: Yeah, that's a nice color. I'll try it on!

Unit 15: Favorites

page 58, CD 2–33
Listening 1

1.
A: Do you travel a lot?
B: Yeah, I do.
A: Which do you prefer—traveling by train or by plane?
B: Well, the thing I like about a train is it's so comfortable. You can get up and walk around. A plane is faster, but you have to stay seated in those uncomfortable seats.

2.
A: Do you prefer living in a house or an apartment?
B: Well, I used to live in a house. I had a nice yard and we had lots of space. But it was too much work, taking care of the yard and all that. An apartment is so much more convenient.

3.
A: Would you rather study American English or British English?
B: Well, they're very similar, but overall I think American English is more useful for me because I watch a lot of American movies and television shows. British English does sound very nice, though.

4.
A: Would you rather work in an office or a department store?
B: Well, I think working in a store would be more interesting. You would get to talk to more people. I think office work would get really boring after a while. I don't like to sit at a desk all day.

5.
A: Which would you rather learn—German or Spanish?
B: Well, German is an interesting language and it's useful in Germany and a few other countries in Europe. But Spanish is used in Spain, Central America, South America, and a lot of places in the U.S. So studying Spanish makes a lot more sense for me!

6.
A: What kinds of music do you like?
B: Well, I like all kinds of music, but I don't care for rock-n-roll very much. It's a little too loud for me. I guess jazz music is my favorite. I really like the piano and strong melodies.

page 59, CD 2–34
Listening 2

1.
A: I love Mexican food. I like it hot and spicy.
B: Yeah, I love it, too!
A: Here. Try some of this. I think you're really going to like it.
B: Mmm. This is delicious. I could eat this every night!

2.
A: I think I'm going to try to get a job in an office when I graduate. I believe I'd really enjoy office work.
B: Really? I don't think I'd like working in an office at all.

3.
A: You know what I like to do when I want to relax—sit down under a tree in a quiet place with a good book.
B: Oh, yeah? I just can't read outdoors. Usually the insects drive me crazy.

4.
A: I guess my favorite kind of music is country. I like music I can sing along with.
B: Me, too. I like country music. Do you like Keith Cannon?
A: Oh, yeah. He's fantastic.

5.
A: In the summer, I play a lot of tennis. I really love it.
B: Do you? I'm not good at tennis, so I hardly ever play it. I prefer to go surfing at the beach in the summer.

6.
A: Well, when I have free time on the weekend, I like to work on my car.
B: Hey, me, too. I just bought an old wreck. Want to come and have a look at it on Saturday?
A: Sure!

page 60, CD 2–35
Listening 3

1.
I really don't like those group tours. You know, the guide picks you up at the hotel every day, and you have to go and see all the sights. I prefer traveling by myself. That way, I can relax. Relaxation is very important to me. I have a very stressful job, so every year I like to spend my two-week vacation lying on the beach and doing nothing.

2.
When I go out to eat, I like to have a nice conversation, and I don't want to be disturbed. That's why I prefer quiet places. I don't like those loud, trendy places. They play loud music in the background, and they're full of such loud people. You have to shout so you can hear each other. It's really annoying!

3.
I prefer staying at one of those small places because I think the service is better. The

people at the front desk remember your name, and the housekeeping people are nice, too. It's like staying in someone's home. I don't like those big tourist places. They might have more facilities, like a gym or a swimming pool. But what I care about most is service.

4.
I don't know how people can stand living downtown. It's too noisy, you can never find parking, and it's dangerous, too. No, I prefer living in the suburbs, for a lot of reasons. For one thing, I like to have a lot of space. That's important to me. I love having a big backyard and a garage for my car. And I also like to have friendly neighbors around me.

5.
Having one is great, especially if you live in a small apartment like I do. That's what I prefer—one just to keep me company. Two would be too hard to take care of. And feeding them would be expensive, too. They could keep each other company while I'm at work, though. But imagine all that cat hair!

6.
I'd prefer a position where I can help people. I know that many people are mainly interested in making a lot of money, but making a lot of money just isn't that important to me. I'd rather do something that is good for everyone and not just myself, even if it doesn't pay very well.

page 61, **CD 2-36**
Pronunciation

1. Do you prefer traveling by train or by plane?
2. Which would you rather learn—German or Spanish?
3. Would you rather work in an office or a department store?
4. Do you prefer living in a house or an apartment?

page 61, **CD 2-37**
Dictation

A: Do you prefer studying at night or in the morning?
B: I prefer studying at night. How about you?
A: I like studying at night, too. Which do you prefer—going out to a movie or watching a DVD at home?
B: I prefer going out to a movie. I like watching movies on a big screen. Which do you like better?
A: I like to watch DVDs at home. It's more comfortable, and I can rewind or pause the movie whenever I want to.

Unit 16: Phone Messages

page 62, **CD 2-38**
Listening 1

1.
Hey, George. This is Sam calling. I just wanted to say how happy I was to hear about your promotion. That's great news. You really deserve it.

2.
Hi, Terry. It's Paula. I am so sorry I wasn't able to come to your party. I heard it was really fun. Unfortunately, I got food poisoning and I just couldn't make it.

3.
Hello, this is Dr. Simpson's office calling for Mrs. Graham. This is just to remind you that you have an appointment on Friday at 2:30.

4.
This is Mr. Kent from Washington High School. I'm calling about Tracy. Unfortunately, she has been absent from school again. Could you please call me back to confirm that she has an excuse to miss school?

5.
Hey, it's Wendy. It's Andrea's birthday on Friday. I was thinking maybe we could organize a surprise party for her. What do you think?

6.
David, this is Kayla. How are you? Are you doing anything on Saturday? There's a great jazz group in town. I know you're into jazz, so I thought you might like to go.

page 63, **CD 2-39**
Listening 2

1.
Rob, this is Olivia calling. It's 2:30. You said you'd meet me at 1:30 in front of the restaurant. Well, I'm not going to wait any longer. And please don't bother calling me again.

2.
Hi, this is Nathan from the computer store. I've been trying to repair your hard drive, but unfortunately, I'm unable to fix it. It looks like you're going to have to get a new hard drive or a new computer. Let me know when you want to come in to pick up your laptop, and I can help you decide what to do next.

3.
Paul, this is Anne. It's 8 p.m., and I'm still tied up at the office, so I don't think I'll be able to join you for dinner tonight. I feel really bad about it, but we'll definitely have dinner tomorrow night. Promise! Bye.

4.
This is Brandon King, from apartment 1201, calling for Kelly. I'm afraid I had a slight accident in the parking lot and did some damage to your car. I'm really sorry about it, but I'm sure that my insurance company will pay for the repairs. Please give me a call when you get in. You can reach me at 555-4026.

5.
Hi, Donna. It's me, Emily! You'll never guess where I am! I'm at the airport with George and the kids. All four of us are here this time. Isn't that great? Hope you've got enough room for us! We'll be at your place by six o'clock. Don't worry about dinner. We can just send out for some pizza—our treat!

6.
Hello, I'm calling for the Burtons. This is Mrs. Parker, from across the street. Your daughter got into my yard today and picked half my flowers. I'd say it's going to cost about $250 to replace them. Not to mention my time and effort. Call me as soon as you get this message. The number is 916-5741.

page 64, **CD 2-40**
Listening 3

1.
A: Hello, Computer Technologies.
B: Hello, could I speak to Pamela Gordon, please?
A: I'm sorry. She's in a meeting right now and won't be available until this afternoon. Can I take a message?
B: Yes, this is Julie calling, from Dr. Beekman's office.
A: Is that J-U-L-I-E or J-U-D-Y?
B: It's Julie, J-U-L-I-E.
A: Got it.
B: Great. Please let her know that we'd like to change her appointment on Thursday from 9:45 to 10:30.
A: All right…needs to change appointment time… And your phone number, please?
B: It's 834-5627.
A: 5-6-2-7.
B: That's right.
A: Okay. I'll pass along the message.

2.
A: Good afternoon. First National Bank.
B: Yes, is Jane Taylor there, please?
A: I'm sorry, she's at lunch right now.
B: Could I leave a message for her?
A: Yes, of course.
B: This is Brian from Jimmy's Shoes.
A: All right. Can I have your phone number?
B: It's 477-3316.
A: 477-3316?
B: That's right. Please tell her that the shoes she ordered are in, and she can pick them up anytime.

A: Okay, Brian. Got it. I'll give her the message just as soon as she gets back from lunch.
B: Thank you.

3.
A: Hello. Chicago Language Center.
B: Yes, can I speak to Mr. Garcia, please?
A: He's teaching a class right now. Would you like to leave a message?
B: Sure, my name is Jeff Leigh. I'm in his 7:30 Spanish class, but I'm not going to be able to make it tonight.
A: Hold on. Is that spelled L-E-E?
B: Actually, it's L-E-I-G-H.
A: Ah, okay.
B: And my number is 627-6082.
A: Is that 627-6082?
B: That's right. Anyway, I can't come to Spanish class tonight because I have to work late. Can you tell Mr. Garcia that, please?
A: Sure.
B: Thanks.

4.
A: Hello. Benny's Cafe.
B: Hi. Is Benny there?
A: No, he just stepped out to the bank.
B: Oh. Could you give him a message, please?
A: Sure.
B: This is Jessica Brown from Pet World.
A: Did you say Pet World?
B: That's right. And I'm Jessica Brown. The number here is 867-5309.
A: 867-5309.
B: Right. He was talking about bringing his cat in for a shampoo and a haircut. Please tell him he can come on Saturday morning, around 11 o'clock.
A: Okay. Come on Saturday morning, 11 a.m., shampoo and haircut. That's for Benny's cat and not for Benny, right?
B: Correct.
A: I'll tell him as soon as he gets back from the bank.
B: Thanks a lot.

page 65, CD 2–41
Pronunciation

1. I'm not going to wait any longer.
2. We're going to go to the mall.
3. I'm not going to be able to make it to class tonight.
4. Do you want to come over?
5. Let me know when you want to come in.
6. I don't want to bother him.

page 65, CD 2–42
Dictation

A: Hi, Michelle. This is Sam. Can I speak with Ben?
B: Hi, Sam. No, I'm sorry. He's not home right now.

A: Do you know when he'll be back?
B: He's going to be out for several hours. Do you want to leave a message?
A: Yeah, thanks. I'm supposed to meet Ben at Cafe Joan for lunch at noon tomorrow. But I have a doctor's appointment, so I'm going to be a few minutes late.
B: Do you know what time you're going to be there?
A: I'll try to get there as soon as I can. I should be there by 12:30.

Unit 17: Past Events

page 66, CD 3–2
Listening 1

1.
I got an invitation to my boss's birthday party on Saturday night.

2.
I thought I'd better get him a nice birthday present, so I bought him a really expensive tie.

3.
When I got to the party, my boss's wife met me at the door and invited me inside.

4.
Then I went in and saw all my friends from work there.

5.
I heard my boss's voice behind me as he came out of the kitchen.

6.
I turned around to say hello, and guess what? He was wearing exactly the same tie as the one I had bought him!

page 67, CD 3–3
Listening 2

1.
Some friends and I were in the elevator going up to my apartment when suddenly the elevator stopped between floors and wouldn't move. We were able to open the doors a little, but we were still stuck!

2.
I went to the airport to pick up my boss. I was so nervous that I wasn't paying attention to what I was doing. After I met him at the arrival terminal, I realized I couldn't remember where I had parked my car. I couldn't believe it! With my boss there and all…I felt so stupid.

3.
When I left for work on Monday morning, I realized I had to walk because I didn't have a dollar bill for the bus. My boss gets angry if I'm late, so I really had to hurry. I was afraid of being fired.

Well, I'd gotten about two blocks from my house when all of a sudden I felt something blow onto my leg. I looked down, and it was a dollar bill!

4.
I wanted to go sailing, but just as I arrived at the lake, a storm broke out and it started to rain. It wasn't a very strong storm, but it was much too cold for sailing.

5.
I was driving down Pleasant Street yesterday. I was singing along with a song on the radio and probably wasn't paying as much attention as I should have been. All of a sudden, a deer ran out in front of my car.

6.
Last weekend, I went out on a date with a friend from my history class. We were at this really nice restaurant, and when the check came, I realized that my wallet was missing. I guess I left it in the taxi after I paid the taxi driver. I didn't know what to do! The check was really expensive!

page 68, CD 3–4
Listening 3

1.
It was a pretty bad snowstorm and the roads weren't in very good condition. I guess I was driving a little too fast and I went into a skid. I couldn't control the car at all! I went off the side of the road and into the snow. Luckily the car wasn't damaged and I wasn't hurt, but I couldn't get the car to move. I just had to stay in it and wait for the tow truck. Finally, after about half an hour, the tow truck arrived and pulled me out.

2.
Yeah, it was pretty scary. We ran into a bad storm and the plane really bumped around. The passengers were pretty scared, and of course all the kids were screaming and crying. It lasted for only 10 minutes, but those 10 minutes felt like an hour! I don't know how the pilot got the airplane out of that storm, but he finally did. And the rest of the flight was perfect.

3.
All I wanted was to get the newspaper. You know how some hotels leave it in front of your door in the morning? Anyway, I stepped out of the room to get it, but the door shut behind me. I tried to open it, but it was locked, and my key was inside the room! I was in my pajamas! Luckily for me, someone from housekeeping came by, and she had a key.

4.
We were staying in this hotel in Thailand when there was a fire. I was so scared when I heard the fire alarm go off! We got

out of the hotel as quickly as we could. The hotel was badly damaged, and some people lost their clothes and money. Fortunately, we were lucky. No guests or staff members were injured.

5.
I was out shopping with a friend when I saw some kids selling raffle tickets to raise money for a charity. It was for a really good cause, so I bought a ticket. I didn't think much more about it. But in the end, I won first prize! It was a good prize, too—a weekend trip for two to New York City!

6.
I was at a restaurant with my wife when this famous movie star sat down at the table next to us. I couldn't believe it! I wanted to ask him for his autograph, but my wife said I should let the man have his dinner in peace. Later, when my wife was in the rest room, I asked the waitress if she would ask the movie star to sign my menu. And believe it or not, he did!

page 69, CD 3-5
Pronunciation

1. We went to the beach on Friday, and just as we arrived, it started to rain.
2. I was walking to work when all of a sudden, I heard someone call my name.
3. I was having a great time, and before I knew it, it was midnight.
4. We waited and waited, and finally, the tow truck arrived.

page 69, CD 3-6
Dictation

A: Did I tell you about what happened to me last Saturday morning?
B: No. What happened?
A: I was walking down the street to get some coffee when suddenly I heard someone call my name. I looked around, but I didn't see anyone I knew.
B: Then what did you do?
A: Well, I thought maybe I imagined it, so I kept walking, and just as I was about to go into the cafe, I heard it again. It was my best friend from elementary school!

Unit 18: Vacations

page 70, CD 3-7
Listening 1

1.
A: What do you think I should do for vacation this summer?
B: Well, you like the beach, and you love hanging out in the sun. Why don't you go to the Caribbean? Or how about the Philippines? Some friends of mine stayed at a beach resort there last summer.
A: Well, I've been to the Caribbean a couple of times, and I always enjoy it. But I've never been to the Philippines. I think that would be fun.

2.
A: I'm not sure where to go for vacation this year.
B: Why don't you go skiing? I had a great time at a ski resort in the mountains last winter. Or how about a jungle trip to the Malaysian National Forest? I did that a couple of years ago, and it was amazing.
A: Well, I just bought some new ski equipment and I'm dying to try it. I have to say that I'm not too excited about the idea of a jungle trip. I don't like bugs, and I bet there would be a lot of them.

3.
A: I'd like to do something really different for my vacation this year.
B: How about a trip down the Nile River? You've never been to Egypt, right? Or maybe you could spend a week in the Australian outback.
A: Hmm. They both sound interesting, but I guess I'd prefer the Australian trip. The Nile River might be just a little too exciting for me.

4.
A: I'd like to do something exciting this vacation. I don't want to just lie around on a beach.
B: How about whitewater rafting down the Colorado River? It takes you right through the Grand Canyon. That's really exciting. Or you could go on a 10-day African safari. I've heard that's a great trip.
A: The safari trip would be fun sometime, but I only have one week. I think I'll do the Grand Canyon trip. Thanks for the tip!

5.
A: Any ideas about where we should go for vacation?
B: I'm thinking about a couple of trips. We could go to Southeast Asia. We'd go to Thailand, Singapore, and Indonesia. The other place I was thinking about going to is China.
A: China! I've never been there. I hear it's fascinating. I've already been to Thailand and Indonesia, so let's go to China.

6.
A: I need help figuring out what to do for my vacation.
B: Well, last year, my friends and I went on a two-week bus tour of Europe. We traveled in nice, comfortable motor coaches and stopped in different cities. We stayed in each city for a day or two, and all our hotel reservations were taken care of.
A: Hmm, that could be fun, but sometimes I get sick when I ride in cars and buses.
B: You could take a train trip across Russia. My sister did that a couple of years ago.
A: Oh, I love trains. And I've never been to Russia.

page 71, CD 3-8
Listening 2

1.
I'm so excited about my trip to Asia. I've never been there before. First, I'm flying to Taipei from the U.S. I'll be spending three days there, because I hear that there's a lot to see and do. I'll also be spending three days in Seoul. I hear the nightlife there is great. Then we go from there to Hong Kong. I'm planning to do lots of shopping there, so I hope two days is enough time to buy everything I need. I would really love to go to Beijing for a few days. But, unfortunately, this tour doesn't go there. After Hong Kong, we'll end up in Thailand for five days. So I guess I won't be able to get to Tokyo or Malaysia on this trip. Oh well. I have to save a few places to visit on my next vacation.

2.
Well, our trip starts off in London. We've got a week there. Then we'll take the bus up to Oxford for two days to see friends. We also wanted to see Cambridge—I hear it's beautiful—but we won't have time this trip. Anyway, then we head to France. We have five days in Paris, which will give us time to see all of those museums. I wish we were going to spend a few days in Germany, too, but this trip doesn't include it. But we do go to Switzerland for three days. I'm really looking forward to that. Then we end up in Italy for the last five days of the tour.

3.
We start off in Los Angeles. We're going to stay there for three days because we want to hit the beach and see the sights. We're not going to go to San Francisco this time, because we've been there before. Then we're off to Denver to visit my sister. We're going to stay there for a week. I hope that's enough time, because I haven't seen her since last Christmas, and we have so much to talk about. We were thinking of going to Chicago after that, but we just don't have time, so it's straight on to Washington, D.C., and New York. We've got two days in Washington and three in New York. We'd really love to get up to Boston for a couple of days, but it probably won't happen. Maybe next time.

page 72, CD 3-9
Listening 3

1.
After graduation, I'm going to fly to Europe and spend a couple of weeks traveling on my own. I'll be in Germany and France, mostly. There are so many things I want

to see and do: museums, restaurants, clubs, cafes, all that stuff. I know my parents worry about me traveling alone, but I just prefer it that way. I guess it's because I want to be free. On those group tours, everything is planned for you.

2.
I'm taking a trip to New Zealand. I hear it's really quiet down there, and the people are really friendly. I want to go to small towns that don't get a lot of tourists. Then I can just check into a cheap hotel and do my own thing. I'm really looking forward to this trip. I guess it's because I need to go somewhere quiet. The city where I live is so noisy, and the people are rude.

3.
When I'm in London, I want to see as many plays and concerts as I can. I also want to go to all the big museums and art galleries there. I'm going to go dancing as often as I can, too. Basically, I want to see and do everything! I really want to make the most of the week I'll be there. I guess it's because I need some excitement. My life has been so boring this year.

4.
I'm going to go to Thailand this winter. I don't want to spend any time in Bangkok because I've been there before. This time, I just want to relax on a nice, quiet beach. I can swim and snorkel every day if I want to, but I don't have to do anything. I just want to relax. I guess it's because I've been so busy at work recently.

5.
I'm spending a month in Mexico. It's going to be great. I don't want to spend any time in Mexico City, though. There are too many tourists there. Instead, I want to go to one of those small, old colonial towns. I guess it's because I want to practice my Spanish. I studied the language for three years in college, and I think I'll get to use it a lot more in a small town.

6.
My friend and I are going to Australia. It's perfect for us because Australia has a lot of cheap hotels for backpackers. They're great places to meet other young people and travelers from all over the world. I'm really excited about this trip. I guess it's because the beaches are great there. I heard the east coast of Australia has some of the best surfing in the world.

page 73, CD 3-10
Pronunciation

1. I'm so excited about my trip.
2. Did you do a lot of fun stuff?
3. You and I should take a trip somewhere.
4. Let's do it!
5. I want to go on vacation soon.
6. Who are you going with?

page 73, CD 3-11
Dictation

A: Didn't you go on vacation last month?
B: Yeah, I did. Joe and I went to a great beach resort in the Caribbean.
A: Wow! Did you do a lot of sightseeing?
B: No. We mostly just relaxed on the beach.
A: That sounds like fun. Did you do anything else?
B: Not really, but we did go out to dinner every night.
A: Were the restaurants good?
B: They were great! And we went to a different one each night.

Unit 19: The News

page 74, CD 3-12
Listening 1

1.
The stock market in New York suffered heavy losses today. And U.S. exports declined for the third month in a row.

2.
Fifteen people were injured in a collision between a tourist bus and a truck on Highway 27 this morning.

3.
Police are investigating the theft of a diamond necklace worth $30,000. The necklace was stolen from the Serina Department Store on Saturday.

4.
Over 25,000 people turned out last night at Flushing Meadows to watch the finals of the U.S. Open tennis tournament.

5.
Seventy-five thousand fans of the group Black Eyed Peas were disappointed last night. The free outdoor concert at Central Park had to be postponed because of heavy rain.

6.
A severe snowstorm caused traffic to come to a stop on all major highways. And the airport was forced to close down most of the morning.

page 75, CD 3-13
Listening 2

1.
A fire destroyed the famous Presidential Hotel last night. Firefighters helped all the hotel guests escape safely from the building, although some people lost their clothes and other belongings. Firefighters say the fire probably started in a guest room, possibly because a guest fell asleep while smoking.

2.
Government health officials have closed down Ocean Gardens, a well-known local seafood restaurant. More than 10 people came down with food poisoning after eating at the restaurant last week. The officials say that the problem was probably caused by contaminated water in the restaurant's fish tanks.

3.
A group of Japanese students was rescued yesterday after being stranded for 10 days in the Australian outback. The trouble started after a vehicle the students were traveling in broke down. They couldn't get cell phone reception where they were, so the students had to survive by eating snakes, insects, and berries, and wait for rescuers to find them. Luckily, the students are all recovering well from their harrowing experience.

4.
Pop singer Jimmy Wild didn't arrive for his concert last night, disappointing over 80,000 fans. A representative of the singer said that he was sick and the concert would be rescheduled for next month. No one knows exactly what Wild's illness was, but sources say he's probably just exhausted because he's been touring for three months straight.

5.
Coast Guard boats are searching for a fishing boat with a crew of four, which has been missing for two days. Shortly after the boat left land, it ran into a very bad storm and sent out a message for help. Several private citizens have volunteered to assist the Coast Guard with their search tomorrow.

6.
And this just in. Bai Yun, the giant panda at the city zoo, has finally given birth to twin cubs. Zoo officials are delighted at this event, since pandas are very rarely born in zoos. Right now, the baby pandas are very small—about the size of mice.

page 76, CD 3-14
Listening 3

1.
A protest by over 5,000 nurses caused major traffic jams downtown yesterday morning. The nurses protested in front of County General Hospital to demand higher pay and an increase in staffing. They say that major budget cuts have resulted in unfair salaries. And because 20% of nursing staff was laid off last month, remaining nurses have to work longer hours and take care of more patients. Later in the day, hospital management promised to consider their demands.

2.
Over 20,000 people so far have visited the national museum to see the collection of

works by the popular Colombian artist, Botero. That is the largest number of visitors the gallery has had for several years. This is the first time that Botero's work has been shown in this area, and the collection includes some of his best-known paintings and sculptures.

3.
Several hundred people are fleeing their homes in Los Angeles, California, because of a forest fire burning out of control in the nearby hills. The fire began five days ago. Hot weather, wind, and a very dry summer are helping the fire spread very quickly. Firefighters have come from as far away as Alaska to help put out the flames.

4.
A customs official at Kennedy Airport was very surprised yesterday when he checked the baggage of a passenger and found over 50 live snakes, some of them very poisonous. The government believes that the passenger was planning to sell the snakes illegally in the U.S. They would have been worth up to $1,000 each. A few snakes escaped from the suitcases, but airport officials say that all of them were caught within an hour.

5.
As a result of the heavy rain over the weekend, city officials fear there may be a flood. Many people living near the river have had to leave their homes. Over 30 families are now homeless. Most of them are staying with friends and relatives. Volunteers worked throughout the weekend to place sandbags along the river.

6.
A spokesperson for two of the country's largest airlines—Northern Airlines and Air International—has announced that the two airlines are discussing a possible merger for next year. If the merger goes ahead and the two companies combine, it could be bad news for travelers. Many business experts think that the new company would certainly raise ticket prices.

page 77, CD 3–15
Pronunciation

1. The woman had two thousand-three hundred-fifty pairs of shoes.
2. He won the election by four hundred-eighty thousand votes.
3. Three thousand-six hundred-eleven people attended the concert.

page 77, CD 3–16
Dictation

A: Did you watch the news last night and see the story about the bank robbery?
B: No, I didn't. What happened?
A: Three men robbed the bank on Fifth Street. They got away with $850,000.
B: Wow! That's a lot of money! I hope the police caught them.
A: Not yet. There's a $15,000 reward for anyone who helps the police capture them!

Unit 20: Opinions

page 78, CD 3–17
Listening 1

1.
I think it's a great way for people to develop pride in their country. It can make people feel good about themselves and their team, and I think that's a very positive thing.

2.
Well, the problem with allowing them in the classroom is they can be distracting for students. If students are texting or going online, they're not paying attention to their classwork. And sometimes they ring during class!

3.
I don't mind them, because a lot of them are really very entertaining. Also, you get to know what new products are available.

4.
I can't see anything useful in it. It's just a huge waste of time, energy, and money. I mean, can you see any point in trying to find out if there's life out there?

5.
Well, if anyone is crazy enough to try it, let them. Who in their right mind would want to jump off a high bridge with just a rope tied around their legs?

6.
Well, they are great company, especially for people who live alone. Having one can help you relax, and possibly even lower your blood pressure.

page 79, CD 3–18
Listening 2

1.
A: Well, space exploration is pretty expensive, but I think it's worth it.
B: Why is that?
A: Well, that's how we learn more about the universe we live in. That's pretty important, isn't it?

2.
A: I can't stand commercials on TV these days. They really annoy me.
B: Oh yeah? Why's that?
A: Because they always interrupt my favorite TV programs, and some of those commercials are really long!

3.
A: I think the Olympic Games are great. I can't wait for the next ones.
B: Really? Why?
A: Well, they encourage an interest in sports and help bring about better international understanding. We need more of that.

4.
A: Every city needs tourism, I think.
B: Why do you think that?
A: Well, because tourism can bring jobs and money to the city. It's a much better way of raising money than taxes.

5.
A: Well, action movies might be fun, but I don't think they are really good for young people.
B: Really? Why do you say that?
A: Because they are way too violent. I never let my kids watch them.

6.
A: If you ask me, people in this city shouldn't be allowed to have those big cars.
B: How come?
A: Because most streets are too small for big cars, and they don't have space for parking.

page 80, CD 3–19
Listening 3

1.
A: I think more attention should be given to studying foreign languages at school. Don't you think so?
B: Sure. Absolutely. I think students should be required to learn a second language. It'll help them get better jobs. I studied Spanish in school, and my Spanish language skills helped me get a great job.

2.
A: I think lawyers have the best jobs in the world. What do you think?
B: I'm not sure I agree. It's true that lawyers make a lot of money, but they also have to work really hard.

3.
A: The shows on TV these days are the worst. Even with 100 channels to choose from, there's nothing to watch.
B: I think it's because most TV shows are written for teenagers. There's nothing for people older than 19 to enjoy.

4.
A: Have you taken the bus lately? It's awful!
B: I know. The last time I took the bus, I had to wait for an hour for it to come. And it was so packed that I couldn't get a seat!

5.
A: Where did you get that skirt? It's so cute.
B: Thanks! I bought it online.
A: Really? I buy books and music online, but I've never bought clothes online. I like to try things on before I buy them.

6.
A: I'm telling you, this rainy weather is driving me crazy. I hate it!
B: I'm actually glad it's finally been raining recently. It's really good for my garden. You should see all the beautiful flowers in bloom.

page 81, CD 3–20
Pronunciation

1. Tourism raises money for cities and creates jobs.
2. Hybrid cars save gas and help the environment.
3. Pets can keep you company, help you relax, and even lower your blood pressure.
4. I think cigarettes are smelly, dirty, and bad for your health.

page 81, CD 3–21
Dictation

A: What do you think about the new mall?
B: I don't know. I haven't shopped there yet. Have you?
A: Yeah, I have. I went last weekend. I liked it a lot. It has a ton of stores, lots of great restaurants, and a big movie theater.
B: Oh, I'll have to check it out soon. It sounds so much better than the old mall.
A: It is. The old mall is boring, dirty, and too small.
B: I agree.

Unit 21: Famous People

page 82, CD 3–22
Listening 1

1.
A: Hey, Lisa, are you free Thursday night? Some friends and I are going to see the new Halle Berry movie. Would you like to come along?
B: Oh, I'd love to go! She's so beautiful. Didn't she win a bunch of beauty pageants when she was younger?
A: Yeah, she did. And she's so talented, too. She's the first African American woman to win the Academy Award for Best Actress.
B: Yeah! That was really exciting.

2.
A: Would you hand me that book on the table?
B: Sure. Here you go. What's it about?
A: It's about Gandhi.
B: Oh, yeah? He helped India become independent, right?
A: Right. It's interesting stuff. He inspired so many people. But did you know he started out as a lawyer?
B: No, I had no idea. So when did he become such an important leader in India?
A: Not until he was in his 40s.

3.
A: You look tired today, Nick. Here. Have a cup of coffee.
B: Thanks. Could you pass me the cream? I was up all night reading the new Stephen King novel.
A: He's the one who writes those horror stories, right?
B: That's right.
A: And haven't they made a lot of his books into movies?
B: Yeah, like *Carrie* and *The Shining*. They're really good, and the books are even better. And really scary, too. This new book is giving me nightmares.

4.
A: How's it going, Amy?
B: Oh, all right. I'm writing a research paper on Leonardo da Vinci, so I've been spending a lot of time in the library.
A: Isn't he the one who painted the Mona Lisa?
B: Yeah. He also did a lot of other great paintings. And he was a scientist and an inventor, too!

5.
A: Hey, Josh! Is that a Bob Marley poster?
B: Yeah. Do you like his music?
A: I sure do. He made reggae music famous all over the world. I love that song of his called "No Woman No Cry." Have you heard that one?
B: Yeah. I downloaded a great version of it just last week. Do you want to hear it?

6.
A: Hey, Jen, do you know where Albert Einstein was from? I need it for this crossword puzzle I'm doing.
B: Well, he's from Germany, originally. That's where he discovered the Theory of Relativity. It completely changed the study of physics.
A: Yeah, I know. I somehow thought he was American.
B: No, but he lived in the United States for a long time. He taught science at Princeton University.

page 83, CD 3–23
Listening 2

A: Good evening and welcome to tonight's edition of Legendary Lives. Our subject this evening is James Dean, actor and hero to the young people of his time. Edward Murray is the author of a new biography of Dean. Good evening, Edward.
B: Hello, Tina.
A: Edward, could you please tell us what you know about Dean's early life.
B: He was born in Indiana in 1931, but his parents moved to California when he was five. He wasn't there long, though, because when his mother passed away just four years later, Jimmy's father sent him back to Indiana to live with his aunt and uncle. While growing up there, he played baseball and basketball, rode horses, and played ice hockey. He used to ride his motorcycle all over the farmers' fields, speeding and chasing cows.
A: So, how did he get into acting?
B: Well, first, he acted in school plays at his high school, where he won a drama award. He also won arts and sports awards in high school, and a speech contest, too. He went to college in California, and that's where he seriously started to get into acting. He did modeling for advertisements and appeared in some TV shows. In 1951, he moved to New York to do more stage acting. In fact, he won an award as "Most Promising Newcomer" for 1954.
A: Well, when did his movie career really start?
B: 1955. His first starring role was in *East of Eden*. He was fabulous! James Dean became a huge success. But the movie that really made him famous was his second one, *Rebel Without a Cause*. That was about teenagers who felt like they didn't fit into society.
A: So, how many more movies did he make?
B: Just one more. Then he died in a car crash in California, in 1955. He loved driving fast. In fact, he was driving his Porsche on his way to take part in a car race when he died.
A: What a tragedy. He only made three movies, so what made him the legend he still is today?
B: Well, I guess his looks, his acting ability, his short life, and maybe the type of character he played in his movies. Many young people saw him as a symbol of American youth.

page 84, CD 3–24
Listening 3

Nelson Mandela, the first African president of South Africa, was born in 1918. His father was an assistant to an important African chief, and as a young boy, Nelson often helped his father. While he listened to people telling the chief about their problems, Mandela decided he wanted to become a lawyer so that he could help his people with their struggle for freedom.

After high school, Mandela studied for a bachelor of law degree. In 1942, he started his political life by joining an organization called the ANC. "ANC" stands for African National Congress. The ANC fought against the laws of the South African government, because these laws made life difficult for black people. Even though most of the country's population was black, the people who ran the government and had all of the power were white. Over the next few years, he and other members of the organization worked hard, and the ANC became a powerful national movement. The group encouraged people to resist the government in a peaceful and non-violent way.

Mandela became deputy president of the ANC in 1952. He was now an important leader of black South Africans. As a lawyer, he helped poor people stay on the land where they lived, instead of being forced to move to areas where the government wanted them to live. He also fought against laws that said that black and white people could not live in the same areas or go to the same schools.

During the early 1960s, the government began watching Mandela carefully, and he was soon arrested. He was sentenced to life in prison in 1962. He was not released from prison until 1990. Even while he was in prison, he inspired people in his own country and others all over the world.

After he was released, Mandela continued to try to achieve the goals he had set almost forty years earlier. In 1994, he became the first democratically elected State President of South Africa. He remained president until he retired in 1999. Today, the world remembers him as South Africa's best known and best loved hero.

page 85, CD 3-25
Pronunciation

1. Would you hand me that book on the table?
2. Could you pass the salt and pepper?
3. What did you do?
4. What would you do if you saw a famous actor?
5. Could you sign your book for me?
6. Did you get his autograph?

page 85, CD 3-26
Dictation

A: So what did you do this weekend?
B: My friends and I went to Los Angeles for the weekend.
A: Oh, really? Did you see anyone famous?
B: Yeah! We saw Leonardo DiCaprio in a cafe and Jackie Chan walking down the street!
A: No way! Did you get their autographs?
B: No. We were too shy to ask. What would you do if you saw someone famous? Would you ask for an autograph?
A: Maybe. I was at a restaurant once, and I took a picture of a big celebrity!

Unit 22: Food and Nutrition

page 86, CD 3-27
Listening 1

1.
I never pay attention to my diet. I eat whatever I want. There's nothing I like more than a big juicy steak for dinner and chocolate cake and ice cream for dessert. Yum!

2.
I'm trying to cut down on cholesterol, so I've stopped eating eggs, cheese, and red meat. I'm eating a lot more fish and chicken.

3.
I'm trying to put on weight. Everyone tells me I'm too thin, so I've started eating a lot more meat and dairy products. It's great. Now I can go out as often as I want for hamburgers and fries.

4.
I've got a real sweet tooth. I love chocolate, candy, and things like that. But I know it isn't healthy, so I've given all that up. Now the only sweets I have are fruit.

page 87, CD 3-28
Listening 2

1.
Well, from what you've been telling me, Mr. Grant, it sounds like you're already eating more vegetables. That's good. But you should definitely eat less cheese. It has a lot of sodium and fat in it. That might explain why your cholesterol level is so high.

2.
I'm glad to hear that you've been eating fish more often, Linda. It's much better for you than meat because it has a lot less fat in it. It will probably help your high blood pressure, too. Now, you should also try to eat more fresh fruit, too, especially berries, like strawberries and blueberries—they're full of antioxidants.

3.
Well, Chris, I think it's great that you've been eating a lot of vegetables. I see you've been having fruit for dessert instead of ice cream, too. That's excellent. But you say you've been feeling tired and weak lately, so you should eat more meat.

4.
Ms. Barton, I'm wondering about all the bread you've been eating. I know you need to lose weight, and sometimes eating a lot of bread makes that very difficult. So, I'd like you to eat less bread for a few weeks. Otherwise, your diet seems pretty well-balanced. You're eating meat, but not too much meat, as well as a lot of fruit and vegetables.

5.
You're right, Mr. O'Brien. You're definitely losing too much weight. It's probably because you haven't been eating meat. Now, even if you don't eat meat, you still need protein. Why don't you try eating more eggs, beans, and cheese? They've got a lot of protein. I'm sure that will help.

6.
Well, Mrs. Johnson, I see here that you've been having stomachaches in the mornings lately. And you say you have cereal with milk for breakfast every day. I think the problem is that the milk is difficult for you to digest. That means you shouldn't eat dairy products, like milk and cheese. I suggest you stop drinking milk for a few months. Try having eggs for breakfast instead of cereal.

page 88, CD 3-29
Listening 3

Cheese is one of the world's oldest foods. It was made by the ancient Egyptians over 3,000 years ago. It is a valuable food, since it contains vitamins and protein. It is used both as a food itself and in many different types of cooking.

There are hundreds of different types of cheese around the world, but they are almost always made from the same thing: milk. Cheese is made from several different kinds of milk, including cow's, sheep's, and goat's milk. Most cheese in the United States is made from cow's milk. Cheese also contains water. A soft cheese, like Brie, contains more water than a hard cheese, like Parmesan.

Cheese is produced through a process called "fermentation." The process of making cheese was probably discovered by chance. Ancient people used to make bags using the skin from an animal's stomach. When they used these skin bags to carry milk, bacteria from the animal's skin reacted with the milk to begin the fermentation. The result was cheese.

Today, cheese making is a very scientific process. First, the milk that will be used is pasteurized, which means that it is heated to remove all bacteria. Then, specially cultivated bacteria, called "cultures," are added to the milk. The milk is kept fairly warm during this period to help the cultures grow. As they grow, the bacteria cultures sometimes release bubbles of carbon dioxide. These bubbles help make the holes in Swiss cheese.

Next, as the milk ripens, it forms a solid substance. This substance is called "curd." The curd is removed, and the water is drained from it. The curd forms the basis of the cheese and may be treated in different ways.

Finally, once it is matured and dried, the cheese is ready to eat.

page 89, CD 3-30
Pronunciation

1. You need to take vitamins.
2. You should eat more vegetables.
3. What types of fruit are you eating?
4. Do you eat a lot of carrots?
5. I've taken two cooking classes.
6. I ate four pieces of pizza!

page 89, CD 3-31
Dictation

A: Hi. I'm Jane, and I'll be your server this evening. What would you like to drink?
B: I'll just have some water, thanks.
A: Okay. And what would you like to eat?
B: Could you tell me what types of vegetables come with the roast chicken?
A: Sure. It comes with peas and carrots.
B: Okay. Then I'd like the roast chicken and vegetables, please. And I'd like a piece of apple pie for dessert.
A: Okay, that's roast chicken and vegetables, and a piece of apple pie.

Unit 23: Predicaments

page 90, CD 3-32
Listening 1

1.
A: You know, I'm in an embarrassing situation. I've got a house guest staying with me. He's been here a while and I don't know when he's going to leave. Do you think I should ask him?
B: Yes, I would if I were you.

2.
A: One of my best friends borrowed $5.00 from me and seems to have forgotten about it. I'm too embarrassed to remind her. I don't think it's worth mentioning, do you?
B: No, it's only a small amount. But next time, make sure you don't lend her any money!

3.
A: This guy at work is always asking me out, and I really don't want to go out with him. Do you think I should tell him I don't like him?
B: Oh, I wouldn't. He'll get the message eventually.

4.
A: You know this friend of mine is always borrowing things from me. One week it's my camera, and the next week it's my stereo. And she always forgets to return them. What do you think I should do?
B: Well, first of all, ask for all your stuff back. And second, don't lend her anything else.

5.
A: My friend invited me to his graduation party, and I completely forgot about it. Maybe I should tell him I wasn't feeling well.
B: Yeah, that's probably the best thing to do. He'd probably be pretty annoyed if he knew you just forgot about it!

6.
A: You know, I have really nice neighbors. The only problem is, they play music really loud at night. It drives me crazy. Do you think I should say something to them about it?
B: Why not? They may not realize it's bothering you.

page 91, CD 3-33
Listening 2

1.
I was looking at some dishes in a department store yesterday when I dropped and broke one. I thought for sure they'd ask me to pay for it, but the salesclerk was nice and said I didn't have to.

2.
I went out for dinner with my girlfriend last night at this Italian restaurant. When I checked the bill, they had charged us for things we hadn't even ordered. I talked to the waiter about it. He apologized and said I didn't have to pay for the things we didn't order. In fact, we got the whole meal for free!

3.
I had a date with my girlfriend last night, but on the way there I got stuck in a traffic jam. I got to the movie theater nearly half an hour late. When I finally arrived, my girlfriend was very upset with me, and we both went home without seeing the movie.

4.
A funny thing happened to me yesterday. This girl came up to me on the street and thought I was the actor Tom Cruise. She even asked me for my autograph. I wasn't really sure what to do! I didn't want to disappoint her, so I went ahead and signed Tom Cruise's name. I hope I did the right thing.

5.
When I got home on Friday, all my friends were waiting inside my apartment. My brother let them in because they wanted to have a surprise party for me to celebrate my birthday. Unfortunately, my apartment was a mess. Can you imagine how I felt? My brother told me they had to spend a half an hour cleaning up when they got there.

6.
There was this guy who sat behind me in class. I'm sure he cheated whenever we had a test. He was always looking over my shoulder. I didn't know what to do about it. Finally, I asked the teacher if I could sit in a different seat. I felt a lot better after that.

page 92, CD 3-34
Listening 3

1.
A: My brother-in-law is okay, but there's one thing he always does that I can't stand.
B: Oh, what's that?
A: Every time he comes to our house, he goes straight to the refrigerator and helps himself to something to eat. The other day he finished two sandwiches that my wife and I were planning to have for lunch.
B: No way!
A: Yeah. At first I didn't want to say anything, but now I've decided that I'm going to speak to my wife about it.

2.
A: Do you know Charles, that guy in our computer class?
B: Sure, I know who you mean.
A: Have you noticed his breath? It can be pretty awful sometimes. I'm surprised someone hasn't spoken to him about it. But I guess it's an awkward thing to mention to someone.
B: Right. I know what you mean.
A: Hey! Maybe I should send him an anonymous note about it. That's a nice way of handling it, don't you think?
B: It sounds good to me.

3.
A: My aunt is staying with us this week. My parents gave her the bedroom right next to mine, and she snores really loudly. It's impossible to sleep at night.
B: You mean it's that loud?
A: Oh, it's horrible! And when I told my parents about it, they didn't help me at all.
B: That sounds frustrating.
A: You bet it is. I guess I'll have to sleep in a different room while she's here.

4.

A: Did I tell you that Lisa borrowed some money from me? She got in a traffic accident and the repairs to her car were really expensive.
B: How much money did you lend her?
A: A thousand dollars.
B: Wow! Has she paid you back yet?
A: Not yet. She's waiting for some money from the insurance company. I guess I'll just have to wait until she gets it.

5.

A: My cousin is acting weird these days. He's depressed, and he talks to himself all the time. He probably needs to see someone about it. Maybe a psychologist or something.
B: You sound pretty worried.
A: I am. I'm going to talk to his parents about it. I don't think they're aware of the problem because they don't see him very often.

6.

A: Do you know that when I got home from work today, that guy next door had parked his car in my parking space again?
B: Really? I thought everyone was supposed to park in their own parking spaces.
A: They are. You know, I hate having problems with my neighbors, but this is the third or fourth time this has happened. I'm going to call the building manager and ask him to do something about it.

page 93, CD 3–35
Pronunciation

1. We have house guests this weekend.
2. I got stuck in a traffic jam.
3. Her classmate is preparing a presentation for tomorrow.
4. My grandparents are sleeping in my bedroom.

page 93, CD 3–36
Dictation

A: What's wrong? You look exhausted.
B: I am. I have a house guest staying with me right now. He's a friend from my English class. He was going to stay for a week, but he's been here for four weeks now.
A: Oh, no! Why has he been staying with you for so long?
B: Well, there was a fire in his apartment building, so he has to find a new place to stay. The problem is, he can't afford to pay the deposit for a new place until he gets money from the insurance company.
A: That's terrible. The poor guy.

Unit 24: Global Issues

page 94, CD 3–37
Listening 1

1.
Well, the government has done quite a bit to reduce water pollution. It's certainly better than it used to be. Now we have to do something about air pollution, which is still pretty bad.

2.
Crime is a growing problem in the country right now. Sometimes it's because people are unemployed. I think what we really have to do is reduce unemployment. That should help the crime problem.

3.
The subway and bus services have definitely got to improve. But the government should really focus on improving conditions for people in the cities. So many people need better places to live and the problem is getting worse.

4.
One of the biggest issues we're facing right now is unemployment. If people can't work, they can't spend any money, and then the whole economy continues to suffer. The government really needs to help create more jobs.

5.
Parking downtown is so expensive, and there's so much traffic on the streets in the morning with so many people trying to get to work. We need a new subway system to make it easier for people to get to work so we don't have to drive our cars all the time.

6.
There has been an increase in life span throughout the world. People live longer now because of the availability of medicine and clean water. We need to make sure this continues.

page 95, CD 3–38
Listening 2

1.
I grew up around here, and the river has always been really polluted. Industries were dumping all sorts of chemicals and waste into the water, so the river really smelled bad. You wouldn't even think of swimming in it. Well, I decided to do something about it. My neighbors and I wrote a letter to the mayor asking him to force these industries to clean up the river. I really hope the government listens to us and takes action.

2.
Over the last few years we've been having much hotter summers and warmer winters. When I was a kid here, we used to have a lot of fluffy, white snow in the winter. Now we don't get that. And there hasn't been much rain for a couple of years. I guess this is the effect of that global warming I keep hearing about in the news. That's why we've decided to move to Chicago. There's plenty of snow and rain up there!

3.
When did the world get so crazy? That's what I'd like to know. For years, I thought everything was fine. Now all I read about in the newspaper is countries fighting each other, dropping bombs, and terrible things like that. You know what I did about it? I stopped reading the newspaper. Now, whenever I want to read something, I just pick up one of those sports magazines. No bad news in there!

4.
It's almost impossible to get across the city in less than an hour and a half during rush hour. There are too many cars on the roads. There are only two freeways, and they just can't handle all the traffic. The only thing that moves quickly in this city is the subway. That's why I took an apartment right next to the subway station.

5.
One of the biggest problems we face is garbage. Where can we put it all? In the past, everything used to get buried in giant landfills, but in many countries today, the landfills are full and there is no room to start new ones. That's why I've decided to try to create less garbage. I buy fewer packaged foods now. For example, instead of buying frozen prepared dinners in plastic trays and cardboard boxes, I buy fresh meats and produce. I also take my own cup to the coffee shop so I don't have to use paper cups. Creating less garbage is really the only solution.

6.
In the future, everyone will have to live in giant high-rise buildings if they want to live in cities. These new buildings might be a hundred stories tall, or more. If cities keep getting bigger, the only way they can expand is upward. I can't stand crowded cities myself. That's why I moved to a small town in the country.

page 96, CD 3–39
Listening 3

In developing countries, more and more people are moving from the country to the cities in order to find work. This is because, in many countries, it is often no longer possible to make a living as a farmer. The result of this movement is the development of what are sometimes called "megacities." These are huge cities with populations of up to 15 million people.

People who move to megacities usually believe that cities have many benefits to offer. They believe that there are more jobs available, and that salaries are much higher than they are in the countryside. They think there will be a lot of new, affordable housing to choose from. And of course, these people are attracted to the exciting, glamorous image of the big city that they have seen on television and in movies. They even expect to live longer and healthier lives in cities, because the health care is better there.

But, in reality, life in these megacities is not always as good as people hope. Jobs are often difficult to find because many of the people who move to the cities have little education and few job skills. As a result, there is a huge supply of unskilled workers to choose from, so salaries are very low. Housing can also be a problem. Many people end up in huge, crowded slums on the outskirts of these cities. And their families may become sick, because even though the health care is better in the cities, it is also much more expensive.

The growing population of megacities causes many other problems for city governments. Air pollution increases, for example, as does crime. Getting rid of garbage is extremely difficult. There is not much space available for public parks and gardens. And as these cities continue to grow, these problems will become even more difficult.

B. I agree that air pollution is a big problem. The air in the city has become so dirty.

page 97, CD 3-40
Pronunciation

1. The man was issued a fine for littering.
2. Pollution is an important issue.
3. How can we decrease air pollution?
4. There's been a decrease in air pollution over the last year.
5. We produce too much trash in this country.
6. The produce at the farmer's market looked so fresh!

page 97, CD 3-41
Dictation

A: There are so many problems in the world today.
B: I know. There's water pollution, air pollution, global warming, unemployment.
A: Yeah, and there's the destruction of the rain forests, traffic problems, housing shortages... It can get depressing if you think about it too much.
B: No kidding. What do you think the biggest issues are?
A: I really think air pollution is the most important issue. If we don't reduce pollution and improve air quality, we'll all have health problems.